SEA THE STARS

THE STORY OF A PERFECT RACEHORSE

SEA THE STAR

Invester

SEA THE STARS

The story of a perfect racehorse

edited by SEAN MAGEE

RACING POST

This edition first published in Great Britain in 2009 by Racing Post Books
Compton, Newbury, Berkshire, RG20 6NL

10 9 8 7 6 5 4 3 2 1

A catalogue record for this book is available from the British Library.

ISBN 978-1-905156-77-1

Designed by SoapBox
www.soapboxcommunications.co.uk

Printed in the UK by Butler, Tanner and Dennis, Frome

Every effort has been made to fulfil requirements with regard to copyright
material. The publisher will be glad to rectify any omissions at the earliest
opportunity.

www.racingpost.com/shop

Frontispiece: *Sea The Stars and Mick
Kinane going to the start of the 2009
Investec Derby.*

Contents

Preface

SEAN MAGEE

. . . .

T*his book tells the Sea The Stars story as it was reported – and as it was illustrated – through the pages of the* Racing Post. *Access to the* Post's *unique resources of reports, articles, data and photographs affords the opportunity to tell the story of a famous racehorse in a completely new way, as it unfolded rather than from the comfortable viewpoint of historical reflection – the Sea The Stars story in the present tense, as it were, rather than the past tense.*

Racehorse careers, however well planned, are never straightforward, and some of the pieces contain speculation – for example, John Oxx after the Eclipse appearing to rule out the Arc – which events saw unfulfilled. The Racing Post *pieces here have not been altered through the 20-20 vision of hindsight, although where appropriate a tiny number of errors of fact have been silently corrected. The one area where hindsight has been allowed to hold sway is in the analysis of each of Sea The Stars' six Group 1 races in 2009 by Graham Dench, senior editor on* Raceform: *these pieces have been updated by Graham to take in subsequent races and, in the final section of the book he offers an overall view of Sea The Stars' level of performance. Passages in italics (like this one) are by myself; the rest of the text is by* Racing Post *writers.*

Given the nature of the material there is inevitably the occasional overlap, but basing the book on reports as they were first filed does lend a special immediacy, and it can be revealing to register how the story changes as the months go on.

The book could not have been published as quickly as it has been without the cooperation of many people, notably John Oxx and his family and the staff at Currabeg; John Clarke at the Irish National Stud; Des Leadon; Vanessa Mallinson and

Raymond Laurie; the long-suffering Julian Brown and James de Wesselow at Racing Post Books; the tireless John Schwartz and Anne Bonson-Johnson at SoapBox; Tim Cox, as always; Edward Whitaker, whose wondrous photographs grace most of these pages (but not pages 18, or 21, where the photos are by Mark Cranham, or page 205, which is by Peter Mooney); and Lee Mottershead, Nancy Sexton and Graham Dench, who wrote pieces specifically for the book. *The project would not have happened at all without the unflagging support of Brough Scott, and it was especially appropriate that Brough and I were watching together at Longchamp at* le moment critique *when Sea The Stars burst through to win the Arc. His email at crack of dawn the following morning read, 'Well – we were there!' And we were.*

Something to celebrate

BROUGH SCOTT

IT had been a long morning, and for us it had been the last one. For them there would still be a fortnight before John Hynes would wrap those blue travel boots round Sea The Stars' forelegs and walk him into the box for the half hour journey across to Gilltown in the last week of October. But the feeling was one of closure, a strange sense of relief and wonder at what they had been through, a realisation that this is what they had been living for.

We had talked to them all. First up was Mick Kinane, then John Hynes, Jeff Houlihan, 'Slim' O'Neill, Alex da Silva, Grace Canniffe, David Boyne, John Clarke, Gary and Craig Witheford and of course to John Oxx himself – that's jockey, groom, travelling head lad, assistant, exercise rider, equine masseuse, farrier, stud manager, primary instructors and trainer. In most Sea The Stars coverage only the first and last get a mention along with owner Christopher Tsui, but here at John Oxx's Currabeg stables on the Kildare edge of the Curragh training grounds was proof of how many hands are needed to deliver a masterpiece onto the turf.

The pride shone out of them, and now that Sea The Stars racing career was over they were at last able to let rip about the titan in their tent. Everyone who has ever got involved with racing dreams of being involved with a top horse, even if only to touch him in passing. For these people the dream had come true. For the last two years they had not been bystanders but actual team players as infinite equine potential flowered into as fine a thoroughbred as ever was foaled. In two weeks Sea The Stars would leave them, but

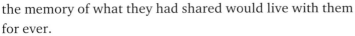

Sea The Stars and John Oxx in October 2009.

the memory of what they had shared would live with them for ever.

Mick Kinane had stacked whole albums of achievement before Sea The Stars swept him past his 50th birthday to a peak even higher than he had been before. All year he had tried to stick to his rigid rule of not comparing one champion with another, of not giving words enough to the press so that they could build of them their own bonfire of vanities. Now he stood on the edge of the golf course across which Sea The Stars walked every morning and relived the sensation of being the top half of the centaur – the immediate promise of the workouts, the exact recall of the races, the realisation of the awesome power he used to have beneath, the crowning fulfilment of his ride along the rail to win the Arc.

It was an overcast morning with a hint of drizzle but nothing could dampen the glow that came tumbling out of recollection, even if at one moment it all got too much for groom John Hynes. Asked what he would miss most, he began to tell us about taking Sea The Stars his apple after work was over and then choked up with the pleasure and the loss of it.

Jeff Houlihan told of racing back from the Arc de Triomphe start and looking in vain for the horse on the big screen as the field turned into the straight. 'Slim' O'Neill spoke of how he himself would ride Sea The Stars round each paddock, even Leopardstown, each big race morning. Alex da Silva, who was once knocked unconscious for a fortnight in a previous job, said 'He my friend' in his best Brazilian and meant it. Grace Canniffe spoke with an expert's insight about Sea The Stars' muscular frame, David Boyne did the same for his feet, and John Clarke talked with an almost doctor-like precision of the day in April 2006 when 64 kilos of healthy bay foal first stood up in the grounds of the Irish National Stud.

Then came a surprise. One of the reasons for producing this book was the realisation of just how little we, let alone the wider public, knew about the detail of getting a great horse into the arena all the way from pedigree planning to the winning post. Because all Sea The Stars' races this year were high profile, and because John Oxx was always so calm and open and reasonable, there was an assumption that we knew most of the story. Yet the more we looked, the more the detail emerged of just how professional an operation John runs beneath the slightly clerical-looking exterior. He even employed Gary Witheford.

The story of how Gary, the former stable lad from Wiltshire, and his riding son Craig 'broke' Sea The Stars in just 12 minutes with his Monty Roberts-style 'pressure and release' method was a typically innovative but unheralded extra.

Through the year John has forced himself to restrain the belief that this is not just greater than all the champions he has trained but even than those he has seen. Now he positively glowed and even broke down for a moment when he recalled Mick Kinane whispering 'This is one of the greats' to him as he unsaddled after the Derby. But it was only for a moment because John wanted to talk of what he had seen, what his team had done, and what incomparable pleasure and pride it was to deal with greatness up close.

He did it because he thinks that in Sea The Stars racing, indeed the whole sporting world, has something to celebrate. So do we. That's what this book is for.

BEGINNINGS

The Sea The Stars story has many alternative beginnings: the day when the mare Urban Sea came into the possession of David Tsui, a Hong Kong businessman; or the Sunday afternoon in October 1993 when Urban Sea won the Prix de l'Arc de Triomphe at Longchamp; or the day when David Tsui's 23-year-old son Christopher, then an economics student in London, went to Epsom Downs to watch All Too Beautiful, a daughter of Urban Sea, finish runner-up – a respectful seven lengths behind the winner – to the soon-to-be-legendary filly Ouija Board in the 2004 Oaks; or 11.20 p.m. on 6 April 2006, when Urban Sea was safely delivered of a bay colt foal by Cape Cross.

That foaling took place at the Irish National Stud, near Tully in County Kildare – where the Irish Horse Museum displays the skeleton of Arkle – and the little colt made an instant impression on the stud's chief executive John Clarke.

'I wasn't there for the actual foaling,' he remembers, 'but as soon as I heard about it the following morning I went to see the foal, and simply loved what I saw. He was a big, strong, very correct, very good-looking colt weighing 141 pounds. There had been no problems with the mare or the foal, and we were absolutely delighted with him. As he grew up, he never had a sick day, never had any accidents or problems, and was easy to handle in every way imaginable. In short, he had a totally uneventful upbringing.'

But the process which led to the moment of that foal's birth in April 2006 was far from uneventful, and to trace that process we must first be introduced to the family who came to consider Sea The Stars 'our baby': the Tsuis.

Previous spread: *Sea The Stars' half brother, a colt foal by Invincible Spirit, at the Irish National Stud with his foster mother Minipen, July 2009.*

'He is our baby': the Tsui family

LEE MOTTERSHEAD

IT WAS the best of times, it was the worst of times. Yet this
is not a tale of two cities, rather a tale of two horses. It is
one that shows that in the ultra-commercial world of Flat
racing, money is not always at the core. Sometimes, the heart
is allowed to rule the head, and for the Tsui – pronounced
'Choi' – family, a precious place in the heart will always be
reserved for two horses, one from the past, one very much in
the present.

The story of the second horse is inextricably linked with
that of the first.

They are tied together by blood, by life and by death. But
for Urban Sea, there would be no Sea The Stars. Had it not
been for Urban Sea, a Miswaki mare who conquered Europe's
Flat racing championship on an October day in 1993, the
sport would have been denied a dynasty of supremely
talented thoroughbreds, the most talented of which is possibly
the best there has ever been. Seventeen years spanned their
respective births, not far short of the amount of time that the
Hong Kong-based Tsui family have been involved in racing
and breeding. At the start of their involvement was Urban
Sea. Now there is Sea The Stars. And thanks to her and thanks
to him, there could be other equine champions to be enjoyed
in the future.

For the Tsuis, 2009 could have been the perfect year.
However, all the good parts bore the wretched imprint of
2 March, when Urban Sea, one of the greatest broodmares
in bloodstock history, died soon after foaling a colt by
Invincible Spirit at the Irish National Stud. Her untimely

passing devastated the Tsuis, but in the ensuing months, the astonishing exploits of her finest offspring allowed them to experience a joy that was overwhelming. When Sea The Stars, carrying the predominantly yellow colours of 28-year-old Christopher Tsui, son of David and Ling, brother of Christine, stormed to an already iconic victory in the Prix de l'Arc de Triomphe, he put the seal on a season the like of which racing has never known. No horse had ever accomplished what the Irish-trained three-year-old colt achieved. Never before had an animal successfully annexed the 2,000 Guineas, Derby and Arc, let alone the Eclipse, International and Irish Champion Stakes as well. It was an unprecedented clean sweep of six Group 1 contests that may never be repeated in our lifetimes. For the Tsuis, it was the defining moments of their racing lives, and it happened at Longchamp, where the seed that sowed those racing lives was planted two decades earlier.

In terms of their involvement in racing and breeding, it is Ling who binds the Tsuis together. Today, she is closely involved with the China Aerospatiale programme as an advisor to Minister Sun Jiadong, the chief architect of the China Lunar Probe Project. In 1989 she was associated with French satellite company Matra, and it was through Matra, and more precisely its chairman, Jean-Luc Lagardere, that Ling was first introduced to racing. As a resident of Hong Kong, where the sport takes place twice a week at the Sha Tin and Happy Valley tracks, Ling knew of racing while at the same time knowing nothing about it. Then Lagardere invited her to France's premier racecourse, Longchamp, where she watched horses competing in the flesh for the very first time.

Not long after, she was watching horses racing in the colours of her husband. The family quickly became addicted to the sport. Soon they had a trainer, Jean Lesbordes, and at one point had as many as 50 horses based in Chantilly, mainly Flat horses but also some jumpers.

Many of their horses were good, some very good indeed. Adieu Au Roi and Take Risks both won Group races for the Tsuis, while Rainbow Dancer brought them a Listed success before being sold to race in the United States, where he became a Grade 1 winner. And while the Tsuis' horses were racing, their son was riding. The ten-year-old Christopher, now a key figure in the family's real estate, manufacturing and international trading concerns, wanted not only to watch but to experience, and so learnt to ride racehorses at Lesbordes' stables. When not enjoying the action at Longchamp, Chantilly or Saint-Cloud, he was often at the yard, developing his skills in the saddle alongside the trainer's son Clement. He loved it.

And love is what the Tsuis quickly felt for Urban Sea. Bought for Fr280,000 at a Deauville auction, she was not one of the all-time greats, but was more than talented enough to race in some of the world's most prestigious Flat races. As a three-year-old, she finished third in the German 1,000 Guineas, sixth in the French Oaks and third in the Prix Vermeille before ending her season at Santa Anita in California and Woodbine in Toronto, where she managed an excellent half-length second to British raider Snurge in the Canadian International.

She continued to race at home and abroad over the following two seasons, winning the Prix Gontaut-Biron at Deauville and the Prix d'Harcourt at Longchamp, while also finishing runner-up in Royal Ascot's Prince of Wales's Stakes, fourth in the Coronation Cup at Epsom, sixth in the Hong Kong Cup at Sha Tin and eighth when flown to Tokyo for the Japan Cup.

In Tokyo, she was almost certainly feeling the effects of what she had done at Longchamp just under two months earlier. Sent off a 37-1 outsider for the 23-runner Prix de l'Arc de Triomphe of 1993, she proceeded to spring one of the biggest shocks in the race's history. Never far from the leaders

Urban Sea lands the 1993 Prix de l'Arc de Triomphe from White Muzzle.

under jockey Eric Saint-Martin, son of the legendary Yves, the then four-year-old Urban Sea began to make her move soon after turning into Longchamp's 500-metre home straight. In front over a furlong from the finish, she resisted all challenges and passed the post a neck and half a length clear of White Muzzle and Opera House.

'Winning the Arc was a childhood memory I will never forget,' says Christopher. 'I was still a child, but I remember the details of that day like it was yesterday. She was truly a great champion.'

She was, but after her racing career was brought to an end by a fetlock injury, she became an even greater champion at stud. The Tsuis could easily have made a fortune by selling Urban Sea as a broodmare prospect, but they instead chose to retain ownership and breed from her themselves under the name Sunderland Holdings. Responsibility for choosing suitable suitors was placed in the hands of Ling. She did a fine job. In chronological order, before her most famous son was born Urban Sea delivered to the world Urban Ocean, Melikah, Galileo, Black Sam Bellamy, All Too Beautiful, My Typhoon, and Cherry Hinton, a septet whose racing achievements are detailed below in Nancy Sexton's account of Sea The Stars' pedigree (which begins on page 27).

Of those horses, none was better than Galileo, who as a sire has already produced a Derby winner in New Approach together with many other top-class horses, including Rip Van Winkle, who found Sea The Stars to be his nemesis through much of 2009. But the horse who would become Urban Sea's greatest legacy to the world was born at the Irish National Stud on 6 April 2006, following a mating with Sheikh Mohammed's stallion Cape Cross. As with all Urban Sea's matings, it was orchestrated by Ling.

It was in part because of Cape Cross' famous daughter Ouija Board that Ling selected the sire. Christopher explains: 'Ouija Board raced her Classic year along with All Too Beautiful. I was invited to watch All Too Beautiful race in the Epsom Oaks, where she finished second, seven lengths behind Ouija Board. My mother and I were very impressed by that race, especially by Ouija Board's speed and turn of foot. She had a lot of endurance and was clearly a very brave filly. By the end of 2004, she had also won the Irish Oaks and Breeders' Cup Filly and Mare Turf. Many had advised my mother to go to more proven stallions, such as Montjeu, but she boldly took the decision to select Cape Cross. She wanted to give more speed to Urban Sea's offspring.'

Time would show that it was an exceptional decision and one that resulted in exactly the outcome that had been desired. And even in the early days it was obvious that the latest foal off the Urban Sea production line was something special.

'Sea The Stars was very solid and big when he was a foal,' recalls Ling. 'My son and I would look at his photos and videos all day on my laptop and every time we did, we remarked on what an attractive colt he was. He really was the most handsome of foals and we were captivated by him. John Clarke at the Irish National Stud asked me if I wanted to put him in the December Sale, but I said: "No, not this one. I love him so much that I will keep him for Christopher." John sent us more photos when the horse was weaned and also told us that he had a good appetite and was very healthy, and from that time I followed his progress from month to month. I told my son that this was his horse and so he had to give him a name worthy of his horse's mother, so he gave him the name Sea (from his mother, Urban Sea) The Stars (because of Galileo). It was a play on words on See The Stars, and one which I liked very much.'

After it was decided to keep Sea The Stars, a trainer was needed, but for Christopher, that choice was not difficult. John Oxx had been responsible for Fairy Of The Night, who won a Tipperary Listed race in Christopher's colours in 2005. The young owner was more than happy with the job done for him by the considerably older trainer and had no doubt where his mother's gift's should be sent. 'I remember that I liked John immediately,' says Christopher. 'He is very calm and never gets excited. He is also very humble, even though he has won so many Group 1 races for His Highness the Aga Khan. So when my mother gave me Sea The Stars, it was an automatic decision for me to send him to John Oxx.'

It did not take long for Oxx to start delivering results. After a promising debut fourth at the Curragh, Sea The Stars landed a Leopardstown maiden and the Group 2 Juddmonte Beresford Stakes at the Curragh, where he kept on well under pressure to see off stablemate Mourayan and Aidan O'Brien's Masterofthehorse. It was a pleasing performance, with no one more pleased than Ling Tsui. She says: 'When he won the Beresford Stakes, he got home by only half a length and people did not pay too much attention to him. Some people even said that it was not a good Group 2 race, but I already liked him so much that I told John Clarke that if he ever won another race as a two-year-old, he could take him on at the Irish National Stud. He agreed, because Sea The Stars had such a good pedigree and is so handsome.'

There were, though, no more two-year-old races for Sea The Stars, just a winter of anticipation. As winter turned to spring, Classic dreams began to burn ever stronger, but in

After the 1993 Arc: Urban Sea's trainer Jean Lesbordes with owner David Tsui and (in red jacket) his son Christopher.

March, with the countdown to their horse's three-year-old debut gathering pace, the Tsuis were dealt two major blows. Sea The Stars suffered a setback, but far, far worse, his mother lost her life.

The subsequent exploits of her son have helped to ease the pain, but for the Tsui family, and especially Ling, the death of Urban Sea hit hard and deep.

'Urban Sea was a very special mare to us,' says Christopher. 'My father travelled all over the world to watch her race, from Hong Kong to Japan, from Santa Anita to Woodbine. After she was retired from racing, mating her to stallions was a task my mother took very seriously. She would spend weeks, indeed months, studying and looking for the best sire. Even though she is very busy with her other duties, this task would always be at the top of her to-do list.

'When Urban Sea died, it was a very difficult time for our family. We are still mourning her and her death has left a void in our lives and the lives of the many people who were connected to her. She was a queen to us and will be dearly missed.

'In her final moments, she was brave until the last minute. She stood up after giving birth so that she could lick her foal, but then she sat down and died peacefully in less than five minutes. It was also only five minutes earlier that my mother was speaking on the phone with John Clarke, who told her that our precious mare had foaled a nice colt and that she and her foal were well. In fact, John asked my mother to go to bed, as he knew that she had only been staying up for news of Urban Sea's foaling.

'My mother only discovered what had happened the next morning. She was devastated, and that's why I prefer to answer any questions about Urban Sea's death. It is simply too difficult for my mother to talk about it. She was the pride and joy of our family, and my mother loved her very much. She was her best friend for the last twenty years.'

The events of the following months could not have not been scripted better. The Tsuis had lost Urban Sea, but they became able to see her through her son. 'When he won the 2,000 Guineas,' remembers Ling, 'it was unexpected because he got a temperature on 17 March. I told John Oxx not to force him. I said to him that I did not mind if the horse did not race in the Guineas, but John thought that this was an important race for him. After he won at Newmarket, I thought he was obviously a good horse, but I also believed that he had the stamina of his mother, so I was not really concerned when everyone started to question his stamina. I had allowed myself to dare to dream that he was very talented. I saw his mother in him.'

But she never once saw him in the flesh. Ling Tsui was not at Newmarket for the 2,000 Guineas, and nor was she at Epsom for the Derby, Sandown for the Eclipse, York for the International, Leopardstown for the Irish Champion or

Longchamp for the Arc. Those who did not know Ling might have assumed that this was because her interest in the horse was minimal, but this could not have been further from the truth. Others suggested that she carried with her a superstition that forced her to stay away from his public appearances. That also contains not one iota of truth.

This is the truth, as Ling explains: 'I rarely go to racecourses because I cannot concentrate and am too nervous. You meet a lot of people on a racecourse and, of course, you need to be sociable, but my heart and my mind are all wrapped up in thoughts of my horse. When a race is approaching, I need to be looking at the pedigrees and race records of our adversaries, but that is not easy at a racecourse. However, when I watch racing at home, I am alone in my office with my TV, laptop and telephone, and I find that I see more of the race like that anyway. What I do want to make clear, though, is that I do not stay away from racecourses because of superstition – my husband and son are more superstitious than me!'

What mother says is correct, particularly with regard to her son. Whenever Christopher was seen at one of Sea The Stars' races in 2009, he was wearing the same suit (except when observing the correct formalities of Derby Day, naturally), tie and watch. Moreover, he brought with him the same seven people on each occasion – which added to himself made a company of eight, a lucky number in Chinese culture – and when the octet dined at Longchamp on Arc day, they dined at table eight. Christopher Tsui became a creature of habit, though thankfully he did not get into a habit of fainting following his horse's triumphs. Just the once, at Sandown in July, was enough.

Christopher, who contrary to many reports is not a nightclub tycoon, says: 'I was next to the parade ring, waiting for the horse to come back, when suddenly I blacked out and fell down. I think I was just too warm and the adrenaline rush got hold of me. It wasn't too big a deal, but now I get it from my mom all the time.

Christopher Tsui at York, August 2009.

23

Before I left for France, she told me: "Don't faint when you go to Longchamp. Have a lot to drink and eat a steak.'"

Perhaps Christopher did have a steak at Longchamp, for at all times he remained vertical. He did get a little carried away – 'I go through uncontrollable emotion. I'd like to be a little calmer and less excitable, but I have no control over it' – but at least there was no need for medics to locate a stretcher and have him carried away. He shouted, he screamed and he jumped up and down a lot, but Christopher survived the Arc, as did his family back home in Hong Kong, where he claims the Tsuis made enough noise to wake their neighbours.

His mother paints a fuller picture. 'When we watched the Arc, which we did on TV and on the internet, we were screaming. My husband watched with Christine and my brother in the living room, but I watched in my office while my mother, who is 84, tried to see the screen over my shoulder. However, I ordered her to close her eyes because I was afraid that if she saw what was happening in the race, she might faint or suffer a heart attack! I cannot explain how we all felt because everyone reacts to things differently. Speaking for myself, I was impressed. I was in complete admiration for our horse. My heart was full of love for him. I was so excited for him and I felt proud when the crowd applauded and showed their genuine appreciation for what he had achieved.

'To me, all of his races were memorable, and it is difficult to choose one in particular. However, the most emotional has to be the Arc, because of the history we have with the race. As my son has said, this is the race that started everything for us.'

And for Sea The Stars, it also finished everything. 'The decision to retire was not difficult,' admits Ling. 'He had completed a full CV and had nothing to prove in racing, so it was the normal decision to let him prove himself at stud. The Breeders' Cup was always an alternative if we decided not to race in the Arc, but after Longchamp, we discussed the possibility of going to America and decided against it. He had already had a very full season and it was time to give him a well deserved rest.'

The rest will not last forever. When the 2010 covering season begins, Sea The Stars will begin his new life as one of the world's most coveted stallions. His mission will be to be as successful at transmitting ability as was his own mother, whose Invincible Spirit foal will one day seek to do Urban Sea proud on the racecourse. As for the racehorse who did her proudest of all, the Tsuis are positively reverential.

'He is a horse that can do everything,' says Christopher. 'He had the speed to win at a mile – in fact John Oxx tells me that he could have won Group 1 sprints if we had targeted them – but he also had the stamina to win at a mile and a half because he did stay very well. And, as we saw at Sandown, York and Leopardstown, he was very comfortable over a mile and a quarter. On top of all that, he looks fantastic and, being a big horse, he is very powerful and imposing. He has the looks of a champion and all the attributes of a great racehorse.'

And for Ling Tsui, who so adored Urban Sea, Sea The Stars has been a priceless gift.

'He means everything to us,' says Ling. 'In Chinese history, emperors were all looking for a "Thousand Miles Horse". The criterion was that the horse had to be calm, strong and tireless. He had to have a champion's spirit and he had to have speed. However, they never mentioned the change of gear, the conformation and the beauty, so Sea The Stars actually has more qualities than the "Thousand Miles Horse" that our emperors so wanted.

'For a breeder and owner, he is the ultimate horse, but for us, he is more that that. My son said that Urban Sea has been his mother's spiritual nourishment, her dream and her consolation. Sea The Stars cannot be measured by his monetary value, for if we sold him, my family would feel so empty. Christopher has described Sea The Stars as part of our family and I agree with him. He is our baby and we really love him.'

SEA THE STARS   B C 6-4-2006

Cape Cross (b 1994)	Green Desert	Danzig	
			Northern Dancer — Nearctic / Natalma
		Danzig	
		Pas de Nom — Admiral's Voyage / Petitioner
	Foreign Courier	Sir Ivor — Sir Gaylord / Attica
		Courtly Dee — Never Bend / Tulle
	Park Appeal	Ahonoora	Lorenzaccio — Klairon / Phoenissa
		Helen Nichols — Martial / Quaker Girl
	Balidaress	Balidar — Will Somers / Violet Bank
		Innocence — Sea Hawk / Novitiate
Urban Sea (ch 1989)	Miswaki	Mr Prospector	Raise A Native — Native Dancer / Raise You
		Gold Digger — Nashua / Sequence
	Hopespringseternal	Buckpasser — Tom Fool / Busanda
		Rose Bower — Princequillo / Lea Lane
	Allegretta	Lombard	Agio — Tantieme / Aralia
		Promised Lady — Prince Chevalier / Belle Sauvage
	Anatevka	Espresso — Acropolis / Babylon
		Almyra — Birkhahn / Alameda

Green Desert

Cape Cross (b 1994)

Foreign Courier

Park Appeal

Ahonoora

Balidaress

Miswaki

Urban Sea (ch 1989)

Hopespringseternal

Allegretta

Lombard

Anatevka

Danzig — Northern Dancer (Nearctic / Natalma); Pas de Nom (Admiral's Voyage / Petitioner)

Foreign Courier — Sir Ivor (Sir Gaylord / Attica); Courtly Dee (Never Bend / Tulle)

Ahonoora — Lorenzaccio (Klairon / Phoenissa); Helen Nichols (Martial / Quaker Girl)

Balidaress — Balidar (Will Somers / Violet Bank); Innocence (Sea Hawk / Novitiate)

Mr Prospector — Raise A Native (Native Dancer / Raise You); Gold Digger (Nashua / Sequence)

Hopespringseternal — Buckpasser (Tom Fool / Busanda); Rose Bower (Princequillo / Lea Lane)

Lombard — Agio (Tantieme / Aralia); Promised Lady (Prince Chevalier / Belle Sauvage)

Anatevka — Espresso (Acropolis / Babylon); Almyra (Birkhahn / Alameda)

Bred by Sunderland Holdings in Ireland

'Regally connected': breeding Sea The Stars

NANCY SEXTON

THERE is a golden rule among trainers to treat every young horse under their care the same, but there must have been a temptation to regard the Cape Cross colt out of Urban Sea that walked into John Oxx's Currabeg yard late in 2007 as something a bit special.

Already a commanding physical specimen in his own right, the youngster was regally connected as a half-brother to Derby winner Galileo, who would go on to land a British and Irish sires' championship the following year, and My Typhoon, winner of the Grade 1 Diana Stakes at Saratoga that summer. To cap it all, his dam Urban Sea was an Arc winner and a half-sister to a 2,000 Guineas winner in King's Best.

There have been many outstanding producers but Urban Sea, who died in March 2009 after foaling an Invincible Spirit colt, thoroughly deserves her place among the top European broodmares of the past 50 years.

Each of her eight runners – by a variety of stallions – has earned black type, three of them at the top level. One, Galileo, is now making his own mark as a stallion.

The daughter of Miswaki is also one of only nine mares since the Second World War to produce two individual British Classic winners.

Bred by the Tsui family's Sunderland Holdings, Sea The Stars was foaled and raised at the Irish National Stud, but his female family is predominantly German, and deeply rooted within Gestut Schlenderhan, which was founded by Baron Edouard von Oppenheim in 1869 and is the oldest privately owned breeding operation in Germany.

However, Schlenderhan's connection with this line of family ceased when Sea The Stars' granddam Allegretta departed to the US after selling for 24,000gns at Tattersalls in December 1981. Up until that point, the stud had cultivated the family to brilliant effect, and even today continues to enjoy success with different branches.

The racing career of Sea The Star's ancestress Asterblute was both brilliant and controversial, as although Schlenderhan's filly captured the 1949 German 1,000 Guineas, Oaks and Derby within the space of two months, the General Stud Book refused to recognise her achievement until volume 29 in June 1977.

The problem lay with Asterblute's sire, Marcel Boussac's brilliant runner Pharis, who was seized by invading German troops from Haras de Fresnay-le-Buffard in France during 1940.

For the next five seasons, Pharis covered mares at Altefeld Stud, then in the hands of the German military, during which time Asterblute was conceived. However, the authorities deemed that all offspring bred during his exile were ineligible for registration, among them Asterblute.

By the time of Asterblute's reinstatement in 1977, she had produced three winners including the stakes-placed pair Adlerflug and Alameda, and it is through the latter's Birkhahn daughter Almyra that Asterblute has had the most impact.

Almyra's 1972 colt Antuco, by the British-trained Grosser Preis von Baden winner Espresso, became the first descendant of Asterblute to score at Group level when taking the Group 3 Oettingen-Rennen, and it was his older sister Anatevka, joint third top-rated filly in Germany of 1972, that helped Asterblute's line to flourish.

Anatevka crossed particularly well with dual German Horse of the Year Lombard, who, as a resident of Schlenderhan, was presented to an abundance of mares by Espresso and Birkhahn, blood which he seemingly worked well with. In addition, the cross of Lombard over Anatevka produced 4x5 inbreeding to Asterblute's dam Aster as well as 4x4 inbreeding to German Derby winner and dual champion sire Alchimist. It was the decision to send Anatevka to Lombard that produced the Deutsches St Leger winner Anno as well as Urban Sea's dam Allegretta, a wiry chestnut filly foaled in Britain in 1978.

Schlenderhan's owner, Baroness Gabrielle von Oppenheim, decided to entrust the filly to Sir Michael Stoute, and the omens looked good when Allegretta won her first two starts as a juvenile over 1m and 1m1f at Leicester and Wolverhampton before running second to Krug in the Zetland Stakes at Newmarket.

Classic aspirations were upheld the following year when Allegretta, who had developed into a tall, light-framed individual, ran second to Leap Lively in the Lingfield Oaks Trial. Although readily brushed aside by three lengths, it seemed that the race would bring Allegretta on, prompting connections to send her to Epsom for the Oaks.

Unfortunately Allegretta turned in an abysmal performance at Epsom, finishing tailed off behind Blue Wind, and it was a similar story three months later in the Park Hill Stakes at Doncaster when, noticeably awash with sweat in the paddock and equipped with blinkers for the first time, she was again unplaced.

Although Allegretta had shown talent during her brief career, she was obviously not the most straightforward, and consequently her next appearance came at the 1981 Tattersalls December Mares Sale, where she was knocked down to Ray Rowley of the Old England Bloodstock Agency for 24,000gns – a fair sum given that the sale's average for fillies in and out of training that year was 21,360gns.

That transaction, however, did not look immediately shrewd. Sent to the US, Allegretta filled the frame only once in three starts and then returned barren in her first two years at stud for her new owner, Big E Farm.

Thus, when she conceived to Irish Castle during her third season, she was given an entry in that year's Keeneland November Sale, where, catalogued in Book 3, she attracted a bid of $55,000 from Horse France: French breeders Marc de Chambure and Michael Henochsberg of Marystead Farm were the successful buyers.

The Irish Castle filly that Allegretta was carrying, Marlene Kelly, won once in France, and she was later followed by the minor winners Irish Allegre and Shadideen. Indeed, when Urban Sea, her 1989 filly by Miswaki, came on to the market at the Agence Francaise August Sale in Deauville in 1990, there was little within Allegretta's produce record to suggest that she would become a noted influence.

Miswaki was already regarded as a high-class sire by the time Urban Sea stepped into the ring, and although the son of Mr Prospector stood at Walmac Farm in Kentucky, he was well known to French breeders, having won the 1980 Prix de la Salamandre for Francois Boutin and Etti Plesch – better known as the owner of Henbit – before producing the high-class French juveniles Waki River, Balawaki and Whakilyric in his early crops.

Like many by Mr Prospector, Miswaki was not short on speed and neither were many of his progeny – he would be later represented by the Prix de l'Abbaye heroine Kistena and the fast two-year-olds Rossini and Abou Zouz. But there were also several runners, such as 1991 US Horse of the Year Black Tie Affair, who excelled over further than 1m. Urban Sea would turn out to be one of them.

It took a bid of just Fr280,000 from trainer Jean Lesbordes to acquire the lean and angular Urban Sea on behalf of a Japanese art dealer, who was declared bankrupt not much later. Luckily for Lesbordes, his Deauville purchases were transferred to Hong Kong businessman David Tsui and Lillian Oung, and when that partnership dissolved in 1992 Tsui purchased the group outright for Fr3,000,000 at the Goffs Arc Sale.

At the time, Urban Sea was already a Listed winner, having landed the Prix de la Seine and Piaget d'Or earlier that season. And prior to the Arc Sale, she had turned in a personal best when narrowly going down to Jolypha and Cunning in the Prix Vermeille.

Over the next year, Urban Sea developed into a tough globe-trotter, appearing at stakes level in Canada, the US, Hong Kong and Britain as well as France. Yet when she lined up for the 1993 Arc she had yet to strike in Group 1 company, even though she arrived at Longchamp in good form, having won her previous two starts including the Group 3 Prix Gontaut-Biron.

Nevertheless, in a field which included King George winner Opera House, Italian invader Misil and Prix du Jockey-Club winner Hernando as well as the crack fillies Intrepidity, Wemyss Bight, User Friendly and Only Royale, Urban Sea appeared over-matched and as a result was dismissed by bookmakers, in some places going off at 40-1.

A bumper field of 23 running over 1m4f on testing ground was always going to lend itself to problems and while several of the runners were inconvenienced by the slow early pace, others were the victim of repeated scrimmaging, especially when the outsider Talloires caused havoc by hanging violently in the straight.

But Urban Sea enjoyed a dream run up the inner under Eric Saint-Martin on her favoured heavy ground, and after hitting the front a furlong out stuck on by a neck from Peter Chapple-Hyam's fast finishing White Muzzle.

Although unable to confirm the form with several of the Arc also-rans on her next outing in the Japan Cup, the durable mare returned as a five-year-old to win the Prix d'Harcourt and finish in the frame for the Prix Ganay and Coronation Cup before injury intervened.

Meanwhile, Allegretta had proved that Urban Sea was no one-hit wonder by producing the Listed-placed Turbaine to Trempolino and the Group 3 winner Allez Les Trois to Riverman.

Seven years after Urban Sea's Arc victory, Allegretta sealed her importance on the breed by producing the brilliant miler King's Best. His victory at Newmarket marked the beginning of an outstanding run of success for the family, which a day later was back in the spotlight following the victory of Urban Sea's second foal Melikah, in the Pretty Polly Stakes. Remarkably, the race was the filly's first public outing.

It did not take long for Miswaki to be regarded as an excellent broodmare sire, and there was evidence that Urban Sea could be an above-average producer when her first foal, the Bering colt Urban Ocean, won the Gallinule Stakes for Aidan O'Brien.

Melikah was from the first crop of Lammtarra, and as the product of two Arc-winning parents had been highly sought after at the 1998 renewal of the Agence Francaise Deauville Sale, eventually falling to Gainsborough Stud Management for a sale record Fr10,000,000.

Following the Pretty Polly, Melikah went on to run third to Love Divine in the Oaks and second to Petrushka in the Irish equivalent, but as talented as she and Urban Ocean were, they paled into comparison against Urban Sea's third foal Galileo, who marked the first of five visits to Sadler's Wells.

The Aidan O'Brien-trained colt won his only juvenile start by 14 lengths at Leopardstown and returned as a three-year-old to take two Derby trials in Ireland in convincing fashion.

At Epsom, he was as dominating as his younger brother would be eight years later, bounding away from 2,000 Guineas winner Golan to win by three-and-a-half lengths. In taking the Epsom Classic, he became one of three grandsons of Allegretta to win a Group 1 race in June 2001, alongside Anabaa Blue, who won the Prix du Jockey-Club, and Anzillero, winner of the Deutschland Preis. Another grandson, the Miswaki colt Tertullian, won the Group 3 Prix de la Porte Maillot for Gestut Schlenderhan.

Galileo's Epsom victory was one of the most visually impressive in Derby history, and he turned in a similarly authoritative winning display in the Irish Derby before taking the King George from a clutch of older horses including Fantastic Light, who turned the tables on him next time out over 1m2f in the Irish Champion Stakes.

But there was more to come. At the end of that season, Galileo's brother Black Sam Bellamy ran third in the Criterium de Saint-Cloud and a year later landed the Gran Premio del Jockey Club. The following season he won the Tattersalls Gold Cup, a month before his sister All Too Beautiful became the third of the mare's offspring to reach the frame in an Epsom Classic when runner-up in the Oaks.

In the meantime, Urban Sea's 2002 produce, a filly from the first crop of Giant's Causeway, had set a world auction record for a foal when selling to Charlotte Weber's Florida-based Live Oak Stud for 1,800,000gns at the Tattersalls December Foal Sale. Later named My Typhoon and trained by Bill Mott in the US, she went on to climb through the Graded stakes ranks before finally annexing a Grade 1 success in the Diana Handicap as a five-year-old.

As a granddaughter of Storm Cat, My Typhoon marked a departure from the tried and tested Sadler's Wells cross, and in 2003 the Tsui family elected to try another different route.

Her mate for that year was Green Desert, who was more a speed influence than any of the other descendants of Northern Dancer she had previously visited.

As it turned out, the resulting produce, Cherry Hinton, showed her best form over 1m2f when runner-up in the Group 3 Blue Wind Stakes en route to a respectable fifth behind Light Shift in the Oaks. Given her high-class form, it was disappointing that she was unable to win, although not as disappointing perhaps as her unraced brother Sea's Legacy, who was sold to Qatar for only 10,000gns as a three-year-old.

The mating of Green Desert's son Cape Cross to Urban Sea

was devised in part following the emergence of the stallion's superstar filly Ouija Board, who had defeated All Too Beautiful by seven lengths in the 2004 Oaks.

Although a good-looking, Group 1-winning miler from the family of Shadayid, Cape Cross had earned breeders' respect the hard way, starting his stud career at a fee of €8,000 at Kildangan Stud in Ireland.

Cape Cross spent his first two seasons on the track with John Gosden, who trained him to run eighth in the 2,000 Guineas and first past the post in the Celebration Mile (later demoted to last). By the end of his three-year-old season he had established himself as a high-class miler who thrived on racing, and consequently it was no surprise to see him race for Godolphin the following year.

However, it was a surprise to see him capture the Lockinge Stakes at 20-1 on his first European start in blue, especially as he had been employed as a pacemaker for Intikhab. But it transpired that the colt was best when able to dominate, and naturally, occasions when Cape Cross was left alone in front did not arise that often; it was again as the Godolphin second string that he triumphed in the Queen Anne Stakes and Celebration Mile as a five-year-old.

Despite falling some way below the leading lights of the Darley roster, Cape Cross's good looks and solid race record meant that he never lacked in support numerically during his early years at stud. And when his first crop of two-year-olds yielded four individual stakes winners, including the Group 2 scorer Mokabra and tough Night's Cross, his popularity soared.

That first crop would also come to include Ouija Board, whose talent and durability not only saw her strike seven times at the top level but also inspire Ling Tsui to nominate Cape Cross for Urban Sea over Montjeu, the choice of several of her advisors.

In addition, by the 2006 season, Cape Cross's stud record also contained Rising Cross, who would go on to run second to Alexandrova in the Oaks, and Group 3 winners Mazuna,

Mac Love and Hazyview, as well as the successful southern hemisphere runners Kindacross, Mikki Street and Seachange. In keeping with his burgeoning reputation, his fee had risen to €50,000.

But as a quick horse from a fast sire line, it would have been difficult to predict exactly what Cape Cross would produce when crossed with a top-class 1m4f mare from a stout German family such as Urban Sea.

What we do know, especially as time has gone on, is that Cape Cross is capable of siring high-class runners over a variety of distances, ranging from the fast Seachange to the Park Hill Stakes winner Rising Cross and Princess Royal Stakes winner Mazuna.

Even though Cape Cross has attracted better quality as his status has grown, Urban Sea is likely to be the best mare he ever

Cape Cross at Dalham Hall Stud.

PROGENY OF URBAN SEA

FOALED	NAME	COLOUR/SEX	SIRE	NOTABLE WINS
1996	Urban Ocean	chestnut colt	Bering	Gallinule Stakes
1997	Melikah	chestnut filly	Lammtarra	Pretty Polly Stakes, 2nd Irish Oaks, 3rd Oaks
1998	Galileo	bay colt	Sadler's Wells	Derby, Irish Derby, King George
1999	Black Sam Bellamy	bay colt	Sadler's Wells	Gran Premio del Jockey Club, Tattersalls Gold Cup
2000	Atticus	bay colt	Sadler's Wells	unraced
2001	All Too Beautiful	bay filly	Sadler's Wells	Middleton Stakes, 2nd Oaks
2002	My Typhoon	chestnut filly	Giant's Causeway	Diana Stakes
2004	Cherry Hinton	bay filly	Green Desert	3rd Blue Wind Stakes
2005	Seas Legacy	bay colt	Green Desert	unraced
2006	Sea The Stars	bay colt	Cape Cross	2,000 Guineas, Derby, Eclipse Stakes, Juddmonte International Stakes, Irish Champion Stakes, Arc
2009		bay colt	Invincible Spirit	

Urban Sea was barren to Sadler's Wells in 2003 and to Shamardal in 2007, and slipped to Pivotal in 2008.

covers. And by producing a horse who could quicken off a high cruising speed without ever being truly extended regardless of distance, the Tsuis' decision to send her to him paid off in spectacular style.

Sea The Stars' race record alone is enough for him to attract support from many of the leading breeders at a fee of €85,000 at the Aga Khan's Gilltown Stud in Ireland, but it is his exceptional looks, temperament, athleticism and family which make him the most desirable stud prospect worldwide.

Galileo's first crop contained no fewer than four European Group 1 winners including the Classic winners Nightime and

Sixties Icon, who led home a sweep of the first three places for
his sire in the 2006 St Leger.

*Galileo and Mick Kinane streak home in
the 2001 Derby.*

They were followed by champion juveniles Teofilo and New
Approach, the latter of whom went on to emulate his sire in
the Derby, and the leading milers Rip Van Winkle – who was
to provide a supporting role in one of Sea The Stars' greatest
moments – and Lush Lashes. Galileo already has a sires'
championship to his credit and it would be no surprise to see him
add another in the near future.

Black Sam Bellamy was popular when he retired to Gestut
Fahrhof in Germany in 2004, but at an opening fee of €7,500 he
appealed to a different level of market. At the time of writing,
he has been represented by three Group 3 winners in Germany,
and currently stands as a dual-purpose sire at Shade Oak Stud in
Shropshire.

Neither Urban Ocean nor Galileo's unraced brother Atticus
have yet to make an impact in the jumps ranks, but Urban Sea's
half-brother King's Best has upheld the family's reputation by

producing the top-class milers Proclamation and Creachadoir. Anabaa Blue has enjoyed his share of success in France as the sire of Arlington Million hero Spirit One, while the German-based Tertullian has already sired two winners of the German 2,000 Guineas in Irian and Aviso.

Certainties are rare in this industry, but it goes without saying that Sea The Stars has more chance than most young stallions to be successful in his second career. We won't know until 2013 whether he will transmit any of his exceptional ability to his offspring, but as a brilliant, beautifully bred descendant of Danzig with the conformation and temperament to match, he has ensured that those involved with him have even more to look forward to.

In the meantime, racegoers can relish the prospect of following Urban Sea's final foal, the son of Invincible Spirit who was born in March 2009.

An Azamour yearling colt, due to go into training with John Oxx, gets a gentle education from the Withefords, father and son – Gary at his head, Craig 'backing' – in October 2009.

S ea The Stars spent the first year and a half of his life growing up in the same lush paddocks where Urban Sea's orphaned son grazed and galloped while his distinguished half brother was setting the racing world alight. But by the beginning of October 2007 it was time for life to start getting serious, and the yearling was boxed up and driven the short distance to John Oxx's yard, Currabeg.

Oxx recalls the new recruit: 'I'd had his year-older half brother by Green Desert, who was a lovely horse but had a few fairly major problems and never raced. But I was not particularly aware of this younger brother until John Clarke phoned me and said that Mrs Tsui would like me to go and look at this fellow at the National Stud: she was not selling him and wanted to put him into training. So I went down to see him for the first time, and he more than fulfilled my expectations. You could not have seen a nicer yearling. He was beautiful – big and strong, very good looking, quite close-coupled; he just looked fantastic, quite outstanding. No breeder could have hoped to breed a nicer looking yearling.'

But a successful racehorse needs more than good looks, and the young colt needed to move to the crucial next phase of his education. At the Irish National Stud, Sea The Stars had been taught basic manners – 'We taught him to walk and stand,' says John Clarke – but it was after he had been transferred to John Oxx's care that breaking-in would be next on the agenda. Not that 'breaking-in' is an appropriate term for the 'pressure and release' method (related to but significantly different from the famous procedure invented by Monty Roberts) pioneered by Wiltshire-based former stable lad Gary Witheford. By Witheford's method, a process which traditionally lasted weeks can be boiled down to twenty minutes – or, as in the case of Sea The Stars, even less.

'I was due to work with 48 yearlings for John Oxx,' he remembers, 'and Sea The Stars was the first one I took out, as he was in box 27 at the Oxx farm, the first box in the row in *the colts' yard. Right from day one I thought he was a lovely horse. Everything he did in his work with me was, "Please, please, please, show me more." With most horses you have to keep asking them to do something until things click and they say, "I get this," but he was much more sensitive than the usual racehorse and learned so quickly.'*

The 'pressure and release' method of educating a horse involves asking the pupil to perform an action – for example as the youngster is sent round the barn on a lungeing rein – and then backing off so that, with the characteristic 'lick and chew' motion of his mouth, he approaches his instructor rather than moving away.

'I took him into the barn and spun him round a couple of times, explains Gary Witheford, 'then put a saddle and bridle on and got him used to the feel of those.'

At this point the Sea The Stars story sees a new player in the form of Gary Witheford's son Craig, who has the distinction of being the first person ever to ride the horse. He started by backing – laying his body across the young horse but not sitting astride him – and then rapidly moved to sitting astride, then riding him round the barn while Gary kept the colt on a lunging rein, then riding round the barn without the lungeing rein – and then, as a final flourish in that life-changing lesson, Craig stood on Sea The Stars' back, in the manner of (but not at the speed of) a circus rider. The point of this last detail was to prevent the horse getting alarmed when a human form suddenly looms above (as opposed to the more usual below) him – say, if a horse is playing up in the starting stalls and a handler clambers onto the frame, thereby suddenly appearing in the sightline of keyed-up horses.

Like his father, Craig Witheford was immediately struck by the quality of this unknown yearling: 'My first impression of him was, "Wow! – what a horse!" Whatever my father asked him to do, it was as if he was a step ahead and he was saying, "Yeah, I've learned that, now let's get on to the next bit." If I thought

The Azamour yearling colt on his learning curve.

about turning, or about going from a trot to a canter, he was ahead of me. He was always so keen, and enjoyed his work.

'For me, he was always a star, and from the very beginning he made me want to be part of his life, however good he might turn out to be. When he won the Guineas I was straight on to my friends to tell them that "my" horse had won the big race, and that I'd been the first person ever to ride him. I taught him everything I knew and my father taught him everything he knew, and we're proud to have been an influence on his life.'

From an early stage at Oxx's yard, Sea The Stars came under the care of John Lynes, who recalls colleague Tony Shanahan pointing out to him the little bone in the colt's forehead, and telling him, that it was supposed to be the sign of a really good horse: 'This was long before he ever ran, but I never forgot that.'

Brought along gently through the winter of 2007-08, the youngster started to show on the gallops that he had ability to match his looks, and by summer 2008 it was time to put that impression to the test. It was time for him to have a race.

THE JUVENILE

CURRAGH (R-H)
Sunday, July 13
OFFICIAL GOING: Straight course - good to yielding; round course - good

---

4002a | **JEBEL ALI STABLES & RACECOURSE EUROPEAN BREEDERS FUND (C & G) MAIDEN** | **7f**

2:05 (2:05) 2-Y-O £9,573 (£2,808; £1,338; £455)

				RPR
1		**Driving Snow**[21] 3302 2-9-0 .... CDHayes 14		90+
		(Kevin Prendergast, Ire) *chsd ldrs: 5th 2 1/2f out: rdn in 2nd over 1f out: led ins fnl f: kpt on wl*	**7/1**[3]	
2	hd	**Black Bear Island (IRE)** 2-9-0 .... JAHeffernan 2		90+
		(A P O'Brien, Ire) *prom: rdn to ld over 1f out: hdd and no ex ins fnl f* **10/1**		
3	¹/2	**Freemantle** 2-9-0 .... JMurtagh 15		88+
		(A P O'Brien, Ire) *in rr of mid-div: prog into 7th 2 1/2f out: rdn in 4th over 1f out: kpt on fnl f*	**6/1**[2]	
4	nk	**Sea The Stars (IRE)** 2-9-0 .... MJKinane 10		88+
		(John M Oxx, Ire) *in rr of mid-div: prog into 7th 2f out: rdn in 5th 1f out: kpt on*	**6/1**[2]	
5	³/4	**Tomas An Tsioda (IRE)**[16] 3463 2-9-0 .... KJManning 16		86+
		(J S Bolger, Ire) *led and disp: led 2f out: rdn and hdd over 1f out: sn no ex*	**9/4**[1]	
6	3	**Double Ex (IRE)**[24] 3185 2-9-0 ....(t) WJLee 12		78
		(T Stack, Ire) *prom: 3rd 2 1/2f out: sn no imp* **14/1**		
7	2 ¹/2	**Indian Ocean (IRE)** 2-9-0 .... CO'Donoghue 17		72
		(A P O'Brien, Ire) *led and disp: hdd 2f out: sn no imp* **12/1**		
8	2 ¹/2	**Daggers Bond (IRE)**[49] 2431 2-9-0 .... FMBerry 8		66
		(Aidan Anthony Howard, Ire) *mid-div: 8th 2f out: kpt on* **20/1**		
9	nk	**Curl Cat (USA)** 2-9-0 .... WJSupple 4		65
		(W McCreery, Ire) *chsd ldrs: no imp fr 2f out* **25/1**		
10	2	**Liebermann (GER)** 2-9-0 .... PJSmullen 11		60
		(D K Weld, Ire) *in rr of mid-div on outer: kpt on fr 2f out* **14/1**		
11	nk	**Shahrafi (IRE)** 2-9-0 .... RPCleary 18		59
		(M Halford, Ire) *hmpd s and s.i.s: sn in rr of mid-div on inner: prog into 8th 1 1/2f out: no ex*	**16/1**	
12	2	**Time 'N' Talent** 2-9-0 .... MCHussey 6		54
		(James Leavy, Ire) *a towards rr* **33/1**		
13	³/4	**Desert Romance (IRE)** 2-9-0 .... PShanahan 5		52
		(Ms F M Crowley, Ire) *mid-div: no imp fr 2f out* **33/1**		
14	4	**Quilca (USA)** 2-9-0 .... DPMcDonogh 13		42
		(Kevin Prendergast, Ire) *a bhd* **16/1**		
15	4 ¹/2	**Cruciform (IRE)** 2-9-0 .... NGMcCullagh 9		31
		(Declan Gillespie, Ire) *a bhd* **33/1**		
16	nk	**Action That (IRE)** 2-8-7 .... ShaneFoley[(7)] 7		30
		(Liam McAteer, Ire) *in rr of mid-div best* **50/1**		
17	2	**Partner (IRE)**[15] 3509 2-8-7 .... EJMcNamara[(7)] 1		25
		(David Marnane, Ire) *chsd ldrs and t.k.h early: wknd fr 2f out* **50/1**		
18	shd	**Conry (IRE)**[58] 2178 2-9-0 .... WMLordan 3		25
		(Patrick Morris) *chsd ldrs: rdn and no imp fr 2f out* **25/1**		

1m 27.27s (0.17) **Going Correction** -0.05s/f (Good)   18 Ran   SP% **138.9**
Speed ratings: **97,96,96,95,95 91,88,85,85,83 82,80,79,75,70 69,67,67**
CSF £78.60 TOTE £4.90: £1.20, £3.00, £2.20, £2.30; DF 96.10.
Owner Lady O'Reilly **Bred** Castlemartin Stud & Skymarc Farm **Trained** Friarstown, Co Kildare

Previous spread: Sea The Stars and Mick Kinane go to post at the Curragh for the colt's first race, 13 July 2008.

In years to come a staple of racing quizzes will be: 'What distinction links Driving Snow, Black Bear Island and Freemantle?' The answer is that they were the only horses ever to beat Sea The Stars in a race, a feat they achieved at the Curragh on Sunday 13 July 2008.

Although there were great expectations of Sea The Stars, the true scale of his potential could not start to be measured until he reached the racecourse, and John Oxx was in no hurry.

'We were not looking for too much for him as a two-year-old,' he recalls. 'We weren't going to wind him up and give him a hard time, as he was a big horse, and still growing. About halfway through the 2008 season, in the late spring and early summer, he started to lengthen. He was a big strong horse, close-coupled, but over the summer he suddenly developed this great length, which of course gave a tremendous reach in his stride. He was changing shape and developing so we didn't want to press him, but he found work so effortless that it was easy to get him to the stage of being fit enough to think about running him.'

The race chosen for Sea The Stars' first racecourse appearance was the Jebel Ali Stables & Racecourse European Breeders' Fund Maiden over seven furlongs at the Curragh – a very short distance from Currabeg – on Irish Oaks day.

With a little over €13,000 to the winning owner, this was far from a humble event, and the previous two runnings had been won by horses who went on to make a major mark. Jim Bolger-trained Teofilo won in 2006 to set in motion an unbeaten five-race juvenile career which culminated in victory in the National Stakes at the Curragh and the Dewhurst Stakes at Newmarket, on both occasions beating Aidan O'Brien-trained hotpot Holy Roman Emperor. Teofilo met with a setback which prevented his ever racing again, but the 2007 winner New Approach – also trained by Bolger – won the National Stakes and Dewhurst and then went on to a brilliant three-year-old career which saw victory in the Derby, Irish Champion Stakes and Champion Stakes.

A field of 18 went to post for the 2008 renewal, and given his recent record in the race it was hardly surprising that Jim Bolger was responsible for the favourite: Tomas An Tsioda at 9-4. Freemantle, one of three runners trained by Aidan O'Brien, was joint-second favourite at 6-1, the same price as Sea The Stars – ridden, as he would be in all his races, by Mick Kinane. The going was officially described as 'Good to yielding'.

Sea The Stars ran a highly encouraging race to finish fourth behind Kevin Prendergast-trained Driving Snow, who won by a head from one of the O'Brien trio Black Bear Island – of whom the Oxx colt would be seeing more – with Freemantle half a length back in third, a neck ahead of Sea The Stars. The Raceform analysis by Tony O'Hehir recorded: 'Sea The Stars, a half brother to Galileo, improved to chase the leaders towards the inside over two furlongs out. He didn't have much room to manoeuvre over a furlong out, before running on quite well in the closing stages.'

Sea The Stars had been beaten, but his jockey was far from discouraged. 'It was the making of the horse,' Kinane reflected much later. 'He wouldn't have been beaten had I not got it wrong on the rails, as going to the furlong marker the run closed in front of me. If he'd got that run, he'd have won. But it was the best thing that could have happened, because in Ireland we don't have a lot of opportunities for a horse that wins his maiden, and they tend to go straight to Group races.'

Driving Snow failed to add to his winning tally in two more races in Ireland in August 2008 and was moved to the USA, where, trained by Todd Pletcher, he was narrowly beaten in the Grade 3 Bourbon Stakes for two-year-olds on turf in October; and in July 2009, now trained by Darrin Miller, he won the Oliver Stakes at Indiana Downs.

Black Bear Island and Freemantle continued under Aidan O'Brien's care as three-year-olds. Black Bear Island – who after the Curragh race had gone on to win at Naas on his only other outing as a juvenile – won the Dante Stakes and

Opposite: *Sea The Stars goes clear of Dark Humour to win the Korean Racing Authority EBF Maiden at Leopardstown.*

....

LEOPARDSTOWN (L-H)
Sunday, August 17
OFFICIAL GOING: Soft to heavy (heavy in places) changing to heavy after race 1 (2.15pm)
The Patrick P.O'Leary, Debutante and Royal Whip Stakes were all rescheduled from the waterlogged Curragh fixture a week earlier.

5129a	**KOREAN RACING AUTHORITY EUROPEAN BREEDERS' FUND (C&G) MAIDEN**	**7f**
	2:15 (2:16) 2-Y-O £9,573 (£2,808; £1,338; £455)	

				RPR
1		**Sea The Stars (IRE)**[35] 4002 2-9-0 .... MJKinane 4		94+
		(John M Oxx, Ire) *prom on inner: led 2f out: rdn and styd on wl fnl f:*		
		easily	2/1[1]	
2	2 ½	**Dark Humour (IRE)**[15] 4656 2-9-0 .... PJSmullen 12		86
		(D K Weld, Ire) *chsd ldrs: 5th travelling wl ent st: rdn and kpt on wout*		
		threatening wnr fr over 1f out	13/2	
3	2 ½	**The Bull Hayes (IRE)**[12] 4714 2-9-0 .... FMBerry 6		82+
		(Mrs John Harrington, Ire) *rrd leaving stalls and v.s.a: prog to 7th 1/2-way:*		
		5th 2f out: styd on wl to go 3rd fnl f	8/1	
4	2	**Vocalised (USA)** 2-9-0 .... KJManning 7		75
		(J S Bolger, Ire) *chsd ldrs: rdn in 3rd ent st: no ex*	5/1[3]	
5	½	**Alyazwa**[15] 4656 2-9-0 82 .... DPMcDonogh 5		73
		(Kevin Prendergast, Ire) *led: rdn and hdd 2f out: no ex*	12/1	
6	4	**Alajan (IRE)** 2-9-0 .... NGMcCullagh 14		63
		(John M Oxx, Ire) *towards rr: kpt on on outer st*	33/1	
7	nk	**Positive Event (IRE)**[63] 3066 2-8-11 .... DJMoran[(3)] 8		63
		(J S Bolger, Ire) *prom: 3rd 1/2-way: no imp fr 2f out*	50/1	
8	2 ½	**Wild And Innocent (IRE)**[20] 4492 2-9-0 .... CDHayes 9		56
		(J T Gorman, Ire) *in rr of mid-div: kpt on same pce st*	50/1	
9	1 ¼	**Bangalore Gold (IRE)** 2-9-0 .... WJSupple 2		53
		(David P Myerscough, Ire) *chsd ldrs: no imp fr 2f out*	40/1	
10	1 ½	**Calm Bay (IRE)**[10] 4802 2-9-0 .... JAHeffernan 10		49
		(H Rogers, Ire) *mid-div: no imp fr 2f out*	33/1	
11	3 ½	**Dylans Secret (IRE)**[32] 4096 2-9-0 .... MCHussey 13		41
		(P J Prendergast, Ire) *a towards rr*	66/1	
12	nk	**Force Of Habit**[51] 3463 2-9-0 .... PShanahan 3		40
		(D K Weld, Ire) *a towards rr*	50/1	
13	nk	**Sirgarfieldsobers (IRE)** 2-9-0 .... JMurtagh 1		39
		(A P O'Brien, Ire) *s.i.s and towards rr: no imp fr 2f out: eased ins fnl f* 9/4[2]		
14	6	**Gracchus (USA)** 2-9-0 .... CO'Donoghue 11		24
		(Noel Meade, Ire) *slowly away and a bhd*	33/1	

1m 34.9s (6.20) **Going Correction** +0.625s/f (Yiel)   **14** Ran   SP% **131.5**
Speed ratings: **98,95,92,90,89 84,84,81,80,78 74,74,73,66**
CSF £16.81 TOTE £3.10: £1.10, £2.10, £2.80; DF 21.90.
Owner Christopher Tsui **Bred** Sunderland Holdings **Trained** Currabeg, Co Kildare

finished runner-up in the Arlington Million in Chicago, while Freemantle, a Tipperary winner towards the close of the 2008 season, failed to win in three outings as a three-year-old: he was beaten only a head by Black Bear Island in the Dante.

Sea The Stars came through his first race well, and five weeks later reappeared in the Korean Racing Authority European Breeders' Fund Maiden over seven furlongs, the first race on a Leopardstown programme run on ground officially described first as 'Soft to heavy (heavy in places)', and then, after the Sea The Stars race, as heavy.

On 18 August 2008, Tony O'Hehir reported for the Post:

Sea The Stars, a half-brother to Galileo, is as short as 12-1 with Ladbrokes but as big as 28-1 with Boylesports for the Derby after his two-and-a-half-length win in the 7f maiden that opened the card at Leopardstown yesterday.

Sea The Stars at Leopardstown.

The son of Cape Cross, who was fourth on his debut at the Curragh, started 2-1 favourite ahead of 9-4 shot Sirgarfieldsobers, a Ballydoyle newcomer and a brother to Authorized.

After boiling over in the preliminaries and becoming upset in the stalls, Sirgarfieldsobers missed the break and never got into contention, finishing 13th of the 14 runners.

Winning trainer John Oxx said: 'Sea The Stars is a nice colt who is half asleep most of the time at home. He handled the ground today, but would prefer it a lot better.

'He's in the National Stakes and the Beresford Stakes, and we'll consider one of those for him.'

Tony O'Hehir's analysis in Raceform *quoted another John Oxx line, which in retrospect was to prove one of the all-time great racing understatements: 'He's not the finished article physically, but is a nice prospect for next year.'*

Of the two possible races mooted by Oxx for next outing of the 'nice prospect', the Group 2 Juddmonte Beresford Stakes would possibly be less fiercely contested than the Group 1 National Stakes, and a further attraction was that the Beresford was a race which had been won by two of Oxx's former superstars in the shape of Alamshar and Azamour. And with the Beresford run over one mile as opposed to the National Stakes over seven furlongs, the former would tell connections more about Sea The Stars' stamina.

On 28 September 2008, Sea The Stars faced five opponents at the Curragh. Half the field were trained by Aidan O'Brien – 11-8 favourite Masterofthehorse (winner of a maiden at Gowran Park), Hail Caesar and Sawtooth Mountain – and two by John Oxx, with the Aga Khan's colt Mourayan seeking to follow up his victory in a Leopardstown maiden in July and a 10-1 chance to do so. Sea The Stars started the well-backed second favourite at 7-4.

Previewing the race, the Racing Post *could hardly contain its enthusiasm: 'Simply put, this is a cracker. Three weeks*

Opposite: *Sea The Stars after his first victory.*

earlier than its usual spot, the Beresford takes on a whole new interest. It is a lot more than a trial, but now there is ample time for the winner to regroup before the Racing Post Trophy or Breeders' Cup in four weeks. When John Oxx won consecutive runnings of the Beresford with Alamshar in 2002 and Azamour in 2003, neither colt ran again that year. That may again be the case if the trainer's Sea The Stars or Mourayan prevails today, but there is now time to consider a trip to Doncaster.

'Trainers are creatures of habit. It is obvious that Oxx has always viewed the Beresford as suitably testing for a future three-year-old star, without being a testing championship race that could leave its mark. Sea The Stars very much fits into the mould of a horse not quite ready for prime time. After a promising debut behind Driving Snow at the Curragh, he was terrific when winning a maiden at Leopardstown, after which Oxx gave a strong idea about his thinking …

'For betting purposes, the Beresford is too tough to call. But what a fascinating race it is, replete with horses who could be much better known by this time next year. Eyes down at 2.20 – we really should not miss this one.'

Again, Tony O'Hehir reports:

Sea The Stars was cut by some firms for the 2009 Derby but failed to excite others after leading a one-two for John Oxx in the Juddmonte Beresford Stakes, and the winning trainer himself expressed some reservations about the half-brother to Gaileo staying the Derby trip.

Ladbrokes left the winner as 12-1 favourite for the Epsom Classic after the Cape Cross colt had beaten Mourayan by half a length. William Hill went 14-1 (from 25), Cashmans are 16-1 (from 20), VCbet 20-1 (from 25), while Sean Graham are unchanged at 20-1.

However, Oxx was in cautious mood after Mick Kinane's mount had made it two wins from three starts and given his

The 2008 Juddmonte Beresford Stakes at the Curragh: Sea The Stars wins from Mourayan (green colours) and Masterofthehorse (far side).

....

trainer his third victory in the 1m Group 2 event, which he won with star colts Alamshar and Azamour in 2002 and 2003 respectively.

He said: 'Sea The Stars travels well and has plenty of speed. He is still developing and won't run again this season. I know he's a half-brother to Galileo, but there is a big difference between Sadler's Wells, the sire of Galileo, and Cape Cross when it comes to stamina, so you couldn't be absolutely certain about him getting a mile and a half.

'His dam Urban Sea did win the Arc, but she was by Miswaki, so it's hard to be certain about the mile and a half for him. We'll just have to see how things go with him over the winter and spring.

'He'll be entered for the 2,000 Guineas and there's also the Irish Guineas to consider. The spring will tell us more, but at this stage I'd be thinking of starting him off over a mile, rather than in a Classic trial over a mile and a quarter.'

Oxx added: 'The ground was a bit dead today and he'd prefer it better. He was on the boil today and didn't run lazily, as he had done in the past.'

Sea The Stars is 25-1 for the Stan James 2,000 Guineas with the Classic sponsors and VCbet.

The winner hit the front early in the final furlong and ran on under pressure to hold the persistent Mourayan, who had led from over two furlongs out.

Masterofthehorse, who was attempting to give Aidan O'Brien his tenth win in the race, was a short head back in third and putting in his best work in the closing stages.

Raceform *noted that Sea The Stars won 'in the style of a smart colt. This was certainly not an extravagant victory, but Oxx is not in the habit of rushing his horses, and there is good reason to believe that the son of Cape Cross will mature into a very smart middle-distance performer. As a half-brother to Galileo, there is a great deal to look forward to, and it was no surprise to learn that he is now finished for the season.'*

And so, with the dreams of Classic glory still very much intact, Sea The Stars returned to Currabeg for the winter.

....

CURRAGH (R-H)
Sunday, September 28
OFFICIAL GOING: Yielding

6316a	JUDDMONTE BERESFORD STKS (GROUP 2)	1m
	2:20 (2:20) 2-Y-O £59,742 (£17,463; £8,272; £2,757)	

				RPR
1		**Sea The Stars (IRE)**[42] [5129] 2-9-1 .... MJKinane 5		112
		(John M Oxx, Ire) *trckd ldrs: 4th 1/2-way: 3rd and hdwy under 1 1/2f out: sn chal: led under 1f out: kpt on wl u.p*	7/4[2]	
2	1/2	**Mourayan (IRE)**[74] [4096] 2-9-1 .... FMBerry 1		111
		(John M Oxx, Ire) *settled 2nd: chal st: led over 2f out: hdd under 1f out: kpt on u.p*	10/1	
3	shd	**Masterofthehorse (IRE)**[54] [4714] 2-9-1 .... JMurtagh 3		111
		(A P O'Brien, Ire) *hld up in rr: 5th and prog on outer over 2f out: cl 4th 1f out: kpt on u.p*	11/8[1]	
4	nk	**Recharge (IRE)**[29] [5523] 2-9-1 .... CDHayes 2		110
		(Kevin Prendergast, Ire) *trckd ldrs: 3rd 1/2-way: 4th early st: rdn 2f out: cl 3rd and chal 1f out: kpt on same pce*	12/1	
5	3	**Hail Caesar (IRE)**[70] [4228] 2-9-1 .... JAHeffernan 6		103
		(A P O'Brien, Ire) *hld up towards rr: last early st: no imp fr under 2f out: one pce*	7/1[3]	
6	3 1/2	**Sawtooth Mountain (USA)**[36] [5296] 2-9-1 101.................. PJSmullen 4		99+
		(A P O'Brien, Ire) *led: rdn and strly pressed ent st: hdd over 2f out: sn wknd*	20/1	

1m 42.3s (0.40) **Going Correction** +0.125s/f (Good)   **6 Ran**   SP% **112.5**
Speed ratings: **103,102,102,102,99 95**
 CSF £18.93 TOTE £3.10: £1.30, £3.50; DF 13.30.
Owner Christopher Tsui **Bred** Sunderland Holdings **Trained** Currabeg, Co Kildare

THE 2,000 GUINEAS

Newmarket, 2 May 2009

3.10 RACE 3 | stanjames.com 2000 Guineas Stakes (201st Running) (Group 1) (Entire Colts & Fillies) (Class 1) Winner £241,840.20 | CH4

1m Row

£400000 guaranteed **For** 3yo, entire colts and fillies **Weights** colts.9st; fillies 8st 11lb **Entries** 88 pay £1100 **1st Forfeit** 29 pay £1600 **2nd Forfeit** 1 pay £30000 **Confirmed** 24 pay £1300 **Penalty value 1st** £241,840.20 **2nd** £91,675.20 **3rd** £45,880.20 **4th** £22,876.20 **5th** £11,459.40 **6th** £5,751

No	Form	Horse	Details	Trainer / Owner	Wt	Jockey	RPR
1 (2)	1216-	**ASHRAM** (IRE) (TT)196 c	ch c Indian Haven-Tara's Girl	Saeed Bin Suroor Godolphin	3 9-0	L Dettori	128
2 (9)	212-2	**CITYSCAPE** (TT)14 D	ch c Selkirk-Tantina	R Charlton K Abdulla	3 9-0	Steve Drowne	126
3 (15)	215-1	**DELEGATOR** (TT)16 CD	b c Dansili-Indian Love Bird	B J Meehan Mrs P Good	3 9-0	Jamie Spencer	128
4 (13)	311-	**EVASIVE** (TT)189 c	ch c Elusive Quality-Canda	Sir Michael Stoute Cheveley Park Stud	3 9-0	Ryan Moore	122
5 (8)	12193-	**FINJAAN** (TT)196 c	b c Royal Applause-Aihufoof	M P Tregoning Hamdan Al Maktoum	3 9-0	T P O'Shea	132
6 (14)	312-	**GAN AMHRAS** (IRE) (TT)216 D	b c Galileo-All's Forgotten	J S Bolger (IRE) Mrs J S Bolger	3 9-0	K J Manning	125
7 (3)	14031-7	**IMPERIAL GUEST** 16	ch c Imperial Dancer-Princess Speedfit	G G Margarson John Guest	3 9-0	John Egan	112
8 (10)	323512-	**LORD SHANAKILL** (USA) 196	b/br c Speightstown-Green Room	K R Burke Mogeely Stud & Mark T Gittins	3 9-0	Jim Crowley	132
9 (12)	11114-	**MASTERCRAFTSMAN** (IRE) (TT)209 BF	ch c Danehill Dancer-Starlight Dreams	A P O'Brien (IRE) D Smith, Mrs J Magnier, M Tabor	3 9-0	P J Smullen	134
10 (11)	361-2	**MONITOR CLOSELY** (IRE) (TT)17	b c Oasis Dream-Independence	P W Chapple-Hyam Lawrie Inman	3 9-0	Alan Munro	117
11 (6)	5451-1	**OCEAN'S MINSTREL** 28 D	b c Pivotal-Minstrel's Dance	J Ryan Ocean Trailers Ltd	3 9-0	Jerry O'Dwyer	109
12 (4)	31231-4	● **ON OUR WAY** (TT)17 CD BF	b c Oasis Dream-Singed	H R A Cecil J R May	3 9-0	T P Queally	121
13 (17)	19419-1	**OUQBA** 17 c	b c Red Ransom-Dancing Mirage	B W Hills Hamdan Al Maktoum	3 9-0	R Hills	126
14 (16)	1810-13	**PURE POETRY** (IRE) 16 D	b c Tagula-Express Logic	R Hannon Mrs J Wood	3 9-0	Richard Hughes	115
15 (5)	117-	**RIP VAN WINKLE** (IRE) (TT)196 BF	b c Galileo-Looking Back	A P O'Brien (IRE) Mrs John Magnier, M Tabor & D Smith	3 9-0	J Murtagh	128
16 (1)	411-	**SEA THE STARS** (IRE) (TT)216 D	b c Cape Cross-Urban Sea	John M Oxx (IRE) Christopher Tsui	3 9-0	M J Kinane	126
17 (7)	311415-	**ZAFISIO** (IRE) (TT)171 D	b c Efisio-Goldthroat	R Curtis H Downs & D Looney	3 9-0	NON-RUNNER	125

● **ON OUR WAY** will run only if suitable ground, states trainer

2008 (15 ran) **Henrythenavigator** (10) A P O'Brien 3 9-0 11/1   J Murtagh RPR123

BETTING FORECAST: 7-2 Rip Van Winkle, 4 Delegator, 5 Mastercraftsman, 9 Sea The Stars, 10 Evasive, Gan Amhras, 14 Cityscape, 20 Ashram, Lord Shanakill, Ouqba, 25 Finjaan, 33 Monitor Closely, 50 On Our Way, 80 Pure Poetry, 200 Imperial Guest, Ocean's Minstrel.

Previous spread: pulling up after the 2,000 Guineas, with the winner (no.16) on the far left.

With the 2,000 Guineas at Newmarket on the first Saturday of May 2009 the probable first target for Sea The Stars, John Oxx commenced fast work with him on the gallops at the beginning of March: 'We started early with him, and things were going great. He was pleasing us in his work and we were ahead of schedule – and then he was due to work on 17 March and he had a temperature of 103. We couldn't believe it. It was just out of the blue. No other horse in the yard had a temperature like that around that time, and it became clear that it was a viral infection. The blood sample was fairly clear but we just walked him for a week, then trotted and then cantered him. From the time he got the temperature to the time he started fast work again was two and a half weeks, the absolute minimum I thought possible. He was a bit down for a day or two but then became quite fresh again, and we were pretty confident that we weren't rushing him.'

Rather than run in one of the traditional Guineas trials, on 17 April he went to Leopardstown racecourse for a gallop with stable companion Arazan, then also a contender for the first English Classic.

'The two of them just quickened up together in the straight and went past the lead horse,' recalls Oxx. 'Sea The Stars needed that bit of work to tell us whether he was fit enough after his setback, and he showed that he was. He and Arazan were a great help to each other.'

Driving to Limerick races shortly after the Leopardstown workout, Mick Kinane shared with Oxx his growing conviction that 'this horse could be the real deal,' but on Friday 24 April, eight days before the Guineas, a serious doubt was sown when Arazan and Sea The Stars worked together at the Curragh. 'The ground was quite soft, and Arazan was too good for Sea The Stars. He just quickened up and finished a couple of lengths in front. It was disappointing that he might not be quite as good as we'd hoped, and there was a bit of a question mark about whether he'd run at Newmarket if the ground was soft.'

On the Tuesday of Guineas week Oxx worked Sea The Stars on the Polytrack gallop: 'I thought that if I took him off grass I'd get a different picture, but he struggled a bit, as there had been a lot of rain, which makes our Polytrack a slowish gallop. I delayed making a decision about the Guineas, and on the Thursday worked him on the wood shaving gallop, which had recently been refurbished. We sent him in to work six furlongs with a companion, and he absolutely flew. I was standing beside the gallop and he just sailed past, going ten lengths clear of the lead horse even though we weren't trying to work him hard, because by that stage he was fit. It was a terrific sight. After his setback the workout on the soft ground was the winning of the Guineas, because it made him struggle a bit and made him work, and he might not have been fit enough for Newmarket without it. It was a tough little build-up to the Guineas.'

It was not only at Currabeg that Sea The Stars was being seriously entertained as a possible Classic winner. On Good Friday the Racing Post's *Pricewise column previewed the 2,000 Guineas, then 22 days away, and noted: 'Sea The Stars was a big, slightly backward juvenile who progressed well and ended up winning the Group 2 Beresford in taking style on his final start. ... [He] could be a really top horse this season, and the 25-1 is too big to miss.'*

By 2,000 Guineas day that 25-1 available in early April had long since shrivelled, and Sea The Stars started at 8-1 for the first Classic, sponsored by bookmaker Stan James.

In a field of fifteen, five horses started at shorter odds than the Oxx-trained colt. Favourite at 3-1 was Brian Meehan-trained Delegator, who had finished fifth in a blanket finish for the 2008 Dewhurst Stakes and sixteen days before the Guineas had won the Craven Stakes over the Guineas course.

The Aidan O'Brien-trained pair Rip Van Winkle (9-2) and Mastercraftsman (7-1), both to play important supporting roles later in the Sea The Stars story, had strong Guineas claims. Rip Van Winkle had won his first two races as a juvenile before finishing seventh in the Dewhurst, while Mastercraftsman had won his first four as a two-year-old, notably the Group 1 National Stakes at the Curragh, and had then run fourth in the Prix Jean-Luc Lagardere at Longchamp. While Mastercraftsman boasted the superior form of the two, O'Brien's first jockey Johnny Murtagh opted to ride Rip Van Winkle at Newmarket.

Half a point shorter than Mastercraftsman on 13-2 was Evasive, trained by Sir Michael Stoute and ridden by Ryan Moore: he had won the Mountgrange Stakes – what was the Horris Hill Stakes – at Newbury in October 2008, while the fifth Guineas runner to start at shorter odds than Sea The Stars was another Irish challenger in Jim Bolger-trained Gan Amhras, runner-up in the Goffs Million at the Curragh as a two-year-old. He started at 15-2.

On paper this was a decent but unspectacular 2,000 Guineas. There was no French challenger and no obvious star – of the field of fifteen, only Mastercraftsman had won a Group 1 race and no runner had an unblemished record. But, as Jon Lees reported the following day in the Racing Post, *this proved to be a race which revealed a true superstar ...*

Sea The Stars and Mick Kinane (dark cap) with Arazan (Fran Berry) in the Leopardstown gallop, 17 April 2009.

Impressive Sea The Stars sets up Classic double bid

JON LEES
3 May 2009

TWENTY years after Nashwan became the last horse to complete the 2,000 Guineas-Derby double, a talent emerged to ignite dreams of the same feat, as Sea The Stars secured the first leg impressively at Newmarket.

The half-brother to 2001 Derby hero Galileo out of a Prix de l'Arc de Triomphe winner boasted a Group 1-winning pedigree, but the sights were raised to a pair of Classics after he had beaten the favourite Delegator in the Stan James-sponsored Guineas.

Without hesitation, trainer John Oxx nominated the Derby as the next target for Sea The Stars after watching him run to a length-and-a-half triumph on the Rowley Mile.

Doubts exist about the stamina of the Cape Cross colt, bred and owned by the Hong Kong-based Tsui family, but after yesterday's performance the bookmakers don't share them. Sea The Stars is now favourite to win at Epsom, at odds as low as 5-2 with Ladbrokes, and a top-priced 5-1 with Coral. He is 10-1 with Skybet to emulate Nijinsky by completing the Triple Crown in the St Leger.

At the beginning of the week Oxx, who also had Arazan entered in the race at that stage, was unsure of his challenge. Sea The Stars, held up by a temperature in March, had failed to work to expectations at the weekend.

Opposite: *Going to post.*

63

Yet on fast ground at Newmarket he gave jockey Mick Kinane no cause for concern as he accelerated past Delegator inside the final furlong, with Gan Amhras third and Rip Van Winkle fourth.

Oxx, landing his first 2,000 Guineas, said: 'When I saw him pick up and pass the pacemaker I knew he would be very hard to beat, because he will run to the line. The uphill finish was going to suit him very well and he won going away.

'We had two good horses for it, Arazan and himself, and we would have fancied the two to be in the frame if they had both turned up. We left the other fellow at home – we just didn't want to run him on fast ground.

'The Derby will be the next race. He had a little bit of a rush to get here. He had a temperature on 17 March, so the five-week interval now will be welcome.

'There is a big debate about whether he gets the trip. With any Guineas winner there is always a debate. You can read the pedigree either way and we'll not know until the day, but I think there is a fair chance of him getting it. If we thought he had no chance, we wouldn't be running.

'He's a horse with a great future. He's got everything – speed, temperament, size, strength. He is a beautiful horse.

'He is such a presence in the yard and is such a pleasure to look at and train. Horses like that get you out of bed in the morning.'

Kinane clinched the more recent of his two Derby victories on Galileo, and his fourth Guineas success proved the jockey, who turns 50 next month, remains a force at the top level despite his years.

He said: 'He is a lovely horse. I've had huge belief in him since last year and whatever he did then, this year was going to be his year. He was way ahead of target and got a viral infection, which really set us back. He was walking for eight days, which is not what you want, so we were a little worried.

'We just got after him to get him here today and last week he did an indifferent piece of work on heavy ground, and we

MICK KINANE

'He jumped out of the stalls, but he was paying more attention to the starter dropping his flag than to the rest of the field, and so I just had to gather his thoughts and get him into a nice position, which he did very quickly. From that point he was travelling beautifully. I knew my only worry with him was just would I get a little flat-footed running into the Dip? I knew that if I was in touch at the rising ground then I was going to come out on top. He had plenty in the tank, and he ran very easily over the line.'

thought we had just piled it on him too quick. The ground brought it all back out in him.

'I want to win the Derby on him now. He is going to be a ride over a longer trip. He is a lovely balanced horse. I don't know if he is going to stay, but he has all the qualities that a top horse has to have. He has a great nature and Epsom won't faze him as an occasion.

'The older you get, the more everyone is waiting for you to fall over, and I am not ready to do that yet.'

Delegator, sent off 3-1 favourite, had quickened to lead over a furlong out but edged to his left before Sea The Stars tackled him.

'I've no complaints,' said trainer Brian Meehan. 'He's proved he's top class and that's what we thought, so we can only be delighted with him.'

Jockey Jamie Spencer said: 'He's run a massive race and there are no excuses. I could have wished for good ground – it got a bit quick for him between the two-furlong marker and the furlong marker.'

JOHN OXX

'He didn't win the Guineas by being off the bridle and out last and just running on and getting up like a Derby horse in the last stride. He won it all the way. After the race we thought, "My God, now isn't that great? He's a half brother to Galileo and he's won the Guineas. The world and his wife will want this fellow at stud." So he had it made when he won, and at the end of the day that's what sets him apart. All his races were significant but the Guineas that started it all off was highly significant.'

A resounding triumph for the virtues of patience and quiet authority

ALASTAIR DOWN
3 May 2009

YOU could not ask for a more taking performance than that of Sea The Stars, who landed the 2,000 Guineas with a perceptible amount in reserve, looking both a truly wonderful prospect and a thoroughly deserving Derby favourite.

John Oxx, tellingly saddling only his second runner in the Guineas, had been making worried noises early in the week after the colt had been forced to work on soft ground and made heavy weather of it.

But when interviewed before the race, he said: 'It may have been a blessing as he had to work a lot harder in the ground and actually seemed to blow up. It could have been a help to him.' Oxx succeeded his father at his yard bang on the Curragh, and the last time I visited there were two 'lads' who had been working there for 42 and 46 years. Such longevity in harness would argue that the Oxx family make for pretty decent employers. John was very much the main man when it came to standing by Johnny Murtagh at the height of his trials and tribulations, and as the ageless Mick Kinane, as relaxed in his work as he has ever been, said here: 'John is a lovely man to work for and it suits me well. We work off the same hymn sheet.'

There will be folk who crab the overall quality of this Guineas, but it looks solid enough given that the first six in

The closing stages: Sea The Stars and Delegator go clear ... and then Sea The Stars goes clearer still.

the betting were the first six home. But the lasting impression from the race was the palpable ease with which Sea The Stars travelled throughout. You could see Kinane knew that he had all the time in the world, and when he pulled him out and saw daylight the colt just ran half-green for a stride before picking up the message and starting to knuckle down and lengthen.

Sea The Stars learned his trade all the way to the line, with Kinane giving him just four far from venomous cracks in the closing stages as Delegator's challenge was comprehensively seen off. If this lacked the instant injection of speed that some seek from a Guineas, it seemed to have a whole lot more to admire for the middle to long term.

Oxx simply would not know how to rush or overface one of his horses. He would rather be seen starkers in Tesco's. A placid man of infinite patience, he is very much a man for letting a horse come to him rather than imposing some artificial timetable that sacrifices the long-term good on the altar of immediate gratification.

He has been eager not to have Sea The Stars 'pigeon-holed' as a Derby horse, and in terms of valuation he has made his point pricelessly with this Guineas win over that commercially crucial mile.

Now Epsom can be the target, and when it comes to stamina for a mile and a half he observed: ' Looking at his pedigree, you could go either way. I think he has a fair chance of getting the trip. He is a very good horse and has speed, which you need at Epsom.'

And speed and the ability to be in the right place are very much Oxx mantras when it comes to the Derby. Many years ago he said to me: 'People go on a lot about whether horses will act at Epsom. But if they travel through the race, then they act.' What he is saying is that the unique demands of the course pull horses who are racing within themselves about the place far less than those already struggling to hold their place.

Sea The Stars travelled in the wide-bottomed seats

Opposite: *Pulling up – ears-back disappointment and ears-pricked satisfaction.*

Taking flight – a bird soars over Newmarket Heath as the legend of Sea The Stars takes off.

throughout in his venture up the Rowley Mile and ate the hill up coming out of the Dip. It is hard to see him being disconcerted by Epsom, and there is an argument that fewer true unremitting stayers are found in the Derby field these days simply because the major breeding operations, who 30 years ago were intent on producing top mile-and-a-half horses, now want ten-furlong horses with speed. The 1m4f trip has moved from optimum wish to maximum tolerated.

Delegator's trainer Brian Meehan will have been disappointed to get chinned and it will be no help telling him that he may have been beaten by an exceptional colt.

He started the day with the Guineas favourite and Derby favourite [Crowded House] and ended it with one beaten and the other deposed by Sea The Stars.

While fully aware that the interpretation of a major race comes down to pounds carried, pace of race, tactics and a myriad of other factors that constitute 'form', sometimes it is

the 'feel' of a performance that strikes you as rock solid.

Here was a colt of established promise overcoming a slightly troubled preparation and winning without turning a hair in the manner of a horse getting better almost as you watched him. He is in the right hands, the steady hands, to shepherd him along and raise him up yet higher. There was something unflashily authoritative about the way Sea The Stars went about his work – a bit like his trainer.

This pair could take us some places in the months to come.

In the unsaddling enclosure – with Lester Piggott, who knows a thing or two about great Guineas winners, looking on from the extreme left. On the right is John Clarke, chief executive of the Irish National Stud, who was to accept the 2,000 Guineas trophy on behalf of the Tsui family.

ANALYSIS

Graham Dench

A solid enough renewal, although on paper it appeared to lack a true star, with just one Group 1 winner in the line-up and just 9lb covering two-thirds of the field on Racing Post Ratings. Although Mastercraftsman, who was officially rated the pick of the 2008 juvenile crop, made the line-up, along with Finjaan and Lord Shanakill, who were both only 3lb behind him, there were some notable absentees, among them Racing Post Trophy winner Crowded House, who was the top two-year-old on RPRs, the Dewhurst winner Intense Focus, the Jean-Luc Lagardere winner Naaqoos, and Shaweel, who was widely expected to be the Godolphin number one.

It had been only recently that SEA THE STARS' connections had started making more encouraging noises about him, his preparation having been held up by a temperature in March and then soft ground at home. However, he came into the race with classy two-year-old form, having been a Group 2 winner on unsuitably soft ground, and he had the pedigree and the physique to step up to another level at three.

It was clear in the preliminaries that he was a colt of real quality and presence, and he put up a performance of sheer class. Drawn on the nearside wing of the field, which raced in one group up the middle of the track, he could soon be seen travelling well, tracking Ocean's Minstrel, and once he made his move and tackled Delegator going to the furlong pole he always looked the stronger stayer. Nothing was making any impression from behind, and as Delegator started to flag in the last 50 yards he strode clear impressively, looking every inch a colt who would do even better when stepped up in trip.

It was no surprise when John Oxx immediately confirmed the Derby as his next race.

Delegator, a really stylish winner of the Craven Stakes, travelled strongly at the back of the field on the opposite flank to Sea The Stars, but having quickened to lead before the furlong marker, he hung left, either feeling the ground or finding his stamina taxed by the uphill finish. He was always coming off second best, but he went on to run Mastercraftsman close in the St James's Palace Stakes, and then, having been sold to Godolphin, to win the Group 2 Celebration Mile at Goodwood.

Gan Amhras was heavily backed once it emerged he was running here rather than stablemate Intense Focus, and he ran a fine race in third. He looked sure to do better over middle distances, but proved bitterly disappointing in both the Derby and the Irish Derby.

Rip Van Winkle, whose only previous defeat came under unsatisfactory circumstances when a hot favourite for the Dewhurst, had his preparation held up by a bruised foot. He came from off the pace and stayed on so well that he only just failed to snatch third. It's impossible to say how much the hold-up cost him, but it cannot have helped. He got closer to Sea The Stars in the Eclipse and the Derby, and won the Sussex Stakes and Queen Elizabeth II Stakes when dropped back to 1m.

His stablemate Mastercraftsman was a dual Group 1 winner at two and had been beaten only in the Jean-Luc Lagardere. He stayed in closer touch, and although he was already in trouble when a bit short of room approaching the furlong pole, he stayed on again. He went on to bolt up in an Irish 2,000 Guineas run in very different conditions, and to win the St James's Palace Stakes on fast ground at Royal Ascot. However, his best performances came over further against Sea The Stars in the Juddmonte International and Irish Champion Stakes.

NEWMARKET (R-H)
Saturday, May 2

OFFICIAL GOING: Good to firm (8.8)
Wind: fresh, behind Weather: bright, partly cloudy, breezy

1675	STANJAMES.COM 2000 GUINEAS STKS (201ST RUNNING) (GROUP 1) (ENTIRE COLTS & FILLIES)	**1m**

3:10 (3:15) (Class 1) 3-Y-O

£241,840 (£91,675; £45,880; £22,876; £11,459; £5,751) Stalls Centre

Form						RPR
411-	**1**		**Sea The Stars (IRE)**[216] [6316] 3-9-0 112.............................. MJKinane 1			124+

(John M Oxx, Ire) *str: w'like: scope: lengthy: lw: hld up in tch: hdwy to trck ldrs gng wl over 2f out: rdn and ev ch fnl 1f out: led jst ins fnl f: r.o wl to assert fnl 50yds* **8/1**

| 15-1 | **2** | 1 ½ | **Delegator**[16] [1300] 3-9-0 115................................... JamieSpencer 15 | | | 120 |

(B J Meehan) *lw: hld up towards rr on outer: hdwy over 2f out: rdn and qcknd to ld over 1f out: sn hung lft u.p: hdd jst ins fnl f: no ex and btn fnl 50yds* **3/1**[1]

| 2- | **3** | ¾ | **Gan Amhras (IRE)**[216] [6317] 3-9-0 111.............................. KJManning 14 | | | 119+ |

(J S Bolger, Ire) *w'like: leggy: chsd ldrs: wnt 2nd and rdn over 2f out: outpcd u.p jst over 1f out: kpt on again fnl 100yds* **15/2**

| 10- | **4** | nk | **Rip Van Winkle (IRE)**[196] [6815] 3-9-0 115.................... JMurtagh 5 | | | 118+ |

(A P O'Brien, Ire) *lw: hld up towards rr: rdn and switching rt looking for run 2f out: drvn and kpt on fnl f: styng on fin: nt pce to rch ldrs* **9/2**[2]

| 114- | **5** | 1 ¾ | **Mastercraftsman (IRE)**[209] [6520] 3-9-0 112.......... PJSmullen 12 | | | 114 |

(A P O'Brien, Ire) *swtg: in tch: rdn and unable qck whn sltly short of room wl over 1f out: sn outpcd: plugged on again ins fnl f* **7/1**

| 311- | **6** | hd | **Evasive**[189] [6979] 3-9-0 108... RyanMoore 13 | | | 113+ |

(Sir Michael Stoute) *lw: chsd ldr tl led 3f out: rdn ent fnl 2f: hdd over 1f out: 3rd and one pce whn short of room jst over 1f out: wknd fnl 100yds* **13/2**[3]

| 0-13 | **7** | 1 ¾ | **Pure Poetry (IRE)**[16] [1300] 3-9-0 101......................... RichardHughes 16 | | | 109 |

(R Hannon) *hld up in rr: rdn and effrt over 2f out: styd on steadily u.p fr over 1f out: nvr pce to threaten ldrs* **66/1**

| 61-2 | **8** | ½ | **Monitor Closely (IRE)**[17] [1291] 3-9-0 101........................ AlanMunro 11 | | | 108 |

(P W Chapple-Hyam) *lw: t.k.h early: in tch tl stdd to rr after 1f: rdn jst over 2f out: kpt on steadily fnl f: nvr trbld ldrs* **28/1**

| 103- | **9** | 2 | **Finjaan**[196] [6815] 3-9-0 118.............................. TPO'Shea 8 | | | 104 |

(M P Tregoning) *swtg: t.k.h: chsd ldrs: ev ch over 2f out: rdn 2f out: wknd qckly over 1f out* **25/1**

| 51-1 | **10** | 1 ¼ | **Ocean's Minstrel**[28] [1118] 3-9-0 102...................... JerryO'Dwyer 6 | | | 101 |

(J Ryan) *led tl 3f out: sn rdn: wknd wl over 1f out* **100/1**

| 10-1 | **11** | 1 | **Ouqba**[17] [1292] 3-9-0 112...................................... RHills 17 | | | 99 |

(B W Hills) *lw: chsd ldrs: rdn and struggling over 2f out: wl hld fnl 1f* **25/1**

| 512- | **12** | 6 | **Lord Shanakill (USA)**[196] [6815] 3-9-0 118....................... JimCrowley 10 | | | 85 |

(K R Burke) *swtg: t.k.h: stdd after s: hld up in rr: effrt and rdn jst over 2f out: drvn and btn wl over 1f out* **14/1**

| 216- | **13** | 1 ¼ | **Ashram (IRE)**[196] [6815] 3-9-0 115.. LDettori 2 | | | 82 |

(Saeed Bin Suroor) *hld up in rr: effrt over 2f out: drvn and wl btn wl over 1f out* **16/1**

| 12-2 | **14** | 5 | **Cityscape**[14] [1354] 3-9-0 110.. SteveDrowne 9 | | | 70 |

(R Charlton) *in tch in midfield: rdn 3f out: sn struggling* **16/1**

| 31-0 | **15** | 49 | **Imperial Guest**[16] [1300] 3-9-0 98.. JohnEgan 3 | | | — |

(G G Margarson) *swtg: a bhd: rdn and toiling over 4f out: t.o fnl 2f* **150/1**

1m 35.88s (-2.72) **Going Correction** +0.075s/f (Good) **15 Ran SP% 124.6**

Speed ratings (Par 113): **116,114,113,113,111 111,109,109,107,106 105,99,97,92,43**

toteswingers: 1&2 £9.70, 1&3 £12.10, 2&3 £9.00 CSF £31.74 TOTE £10.60: £3.10, £1.90, £3.60; EX 49.80 Trifecta £360.30 Pool: £42,004.06 - 86.25 winning units.

Owner Christopher Tsui **Bred** Sunderland Holdings **Trained** Currabeg, Co Kildare

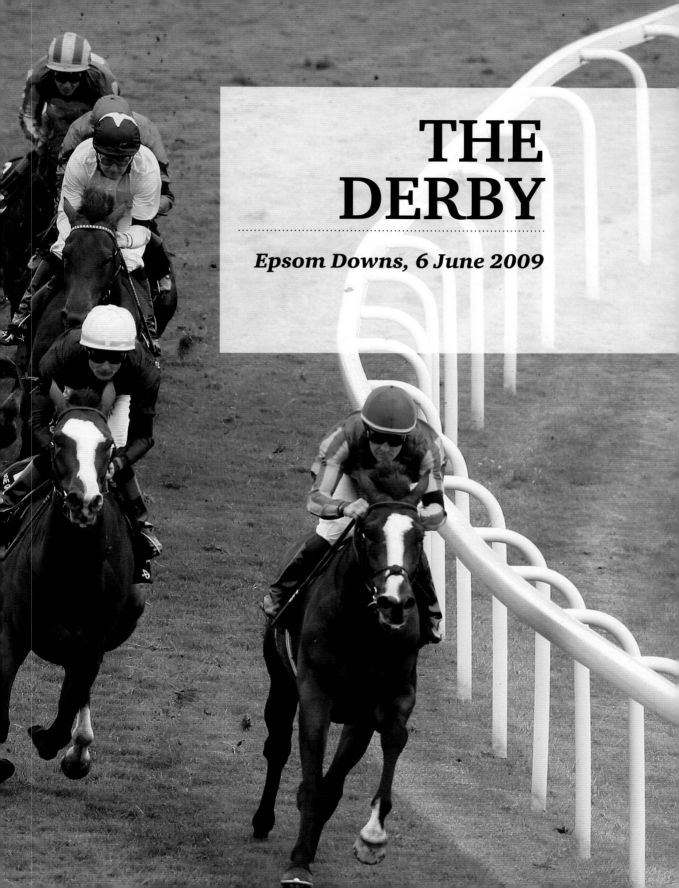

THE DERBY

Epsom Downs, 6 June 2009

3.45
RACE 5

Investec Derby (Class 1, Group 1)

Winner £802,444

TOTE SCOOP6 Leg 6

BBC1

(1m4f10y) **1m4f**

£1,250,000 guaranteed **For** 3yo entire colts & fillies **Entries** 474 pay £325 **1st Forfeit** 138 pay £1,000 **2nd Forfeit** 19 pay £3,000 **Second stage entries** 8 pay £8,000 **Second stage entry acceptors** 1 pay £10,000 **Confirmations** 13 pay £2,500
Penalty value 1st £709,625 **2nd** £269,000 **3rd** £134,625 **4th** £67,125 **5th** £33,625 **6th** £16,875

1 (1)	14-1 **AGE OF AQUARIUS** (IRE) 28	3 9-0	
	b c Galileo-Clara Bow	P J Smullen	
	A P O'Brien (IRE) Mrs Magnier/Tabor/Smith/Mordukhovitch	(124)	
2 (3)	21-31 **BLACK BEAR ISLAND** (IRE) 23	3 9-0	
	b c Sadler's Wells-Kasora	Ryan Moore	
	A P O'Brien (IRE) Mrs John Magnier, M Tabor & D Smith	(134)	
3 (12)	0121-8 **CROWDED HOUSE** 23 [BF]	3 9-0	
	ch c Rainbow Quest-Wiener Wald	Jamie Spencer	
	B J Meehan J P Reddam, Mrs Carmen Burrell, J Harvey	(134)	
4 (5)	4-113 **DEBUSSY** (IRE) 30 [C]	3 9-0	
	b c Diesis-Opera Comique	Jimmy Fortune	
	J H M Gosden H R H Princess Haya Of Jordan	(122)	
5 (10)	11-11 **FAME AND GLORY** 27	3 9-0	
	b c Montjeu-Gryada	J A Heffernan	
	A P O'Brien (IRE) D Smith, Mrs J Magnier, M Tabor	(136)	
6 (6)	312-3 **GAN AMHRAS** (IRE) 35	3 9-0	
	b c Galileo-All's Forgotten	K J Manning	
	J S Bolger (IRE) Mrs J S Bolger	(136)	
7 (7)	3541-41 **GOLDEN SWORD** 30 [D]	3 9-0	
	b c High Chaparral-Sitara	C O'Donoghue	
	A P O'Brien (IRE) M Tabor, D Smith & Mrs John Magnier	(126)	
8 (8)	211-5 **KITE WOOD** (IRE) 23	3 9-0	
	b c Galileo-Kite Mark	L Dettori	
	Saeed Bin Suroor Godolphin	(128)	
9 (2)	2130-2 **MASTEROFTHEHORSE** (IRE) 30 [BF]	3 9-0	
	b c Sadler's Wells-Shouk	Richard Hughes	
	A P O'Brien (IRE) M Tabor, D Smith & Mrs John Magnier	(125)	
10 (11)	21-2 **MONTAFF** 28	3 9-0	
	b c Montjeu-Meshhed	R Hills	
	M R Channon Barry Walters Catering	(121)	
11 (9)	117-4 **RIP VAN WINKLE** (IRE) 35	3 9-0	
	b c Galileo-Looking Back	J Murtagh	
	A P O'Brien (IRE) Mrs John Magnier, M Tabor & D Smith	(135)	
12 (4)	411-1 **SEA THE STARS** (IRE) 35	3 9-0	
	b c Cape Cross-Urban Sea	M J Kinane	
	John M Oxx (IRE) Christopher Tsui	(139)	
13 (13)	21 **SOUTH EASTER** (IRE) 29	3 9-0	
	ch c Galileo-Dance Treat	NON-RUNNER	
	W J Haggas Markus Jooste & Bernard Kantor	(121)	

2008 (16 ran) **New Approach** (3) J S Bolger 3 9-0 5/1   K J Manning RPR126

BETTING FORECAST: 11-4 Sea The Stars, 7-2 Fame And Glory, 4 Rip Van Winkle, 7 Gan Amhras, 8 Black Bear Island, 14 Masterofthehorse, 20 Age Of Aquarius, Crowded House, 25 Kite Wood, 33 Golden Sword, 50 Montaff, 66 Debussy.

Previous spread: Tattenham Corner.

The presentations after the 2,000 Guineas had been made by Lester Piggott, who seized the opportunity to mutter to Mick Kinane as he handed him his trophy, 'Will he stay?' Having won that Classic five times in his riding days – including on two of the greats in Sir Ivor and Nijinsky – Piggott was well aware that the key post-Guineas issue is whether the winner of a top-class race over a mile will have the stamina to follow up in the Derby five weeks later, over a distance half as long again. Both Sir Ivor and Nijinsky had gloriously achieved the double, but could Sea The Stars join such exalted company?

His pedigree boasted strong influences for stamina as well as speed, but for some observers the manner of his Newmarket win raised doubts about his having the requisite staying power, for the simple reason that he had proved himself so fast. Months later, Mick Kinane would smile wryly as he recalled: 'They said he could not win the Guineas because he was a Derby horse. Now they were saying he can't take the Derby because he is a Guineas winner … '

For his part, John Oxx was 'always a little concerned. I never took it for granted, even though Mick was confident. All the same, I was probably a little more confident than I was letting on, and at the back of my mind I thought he'd probably get the trip.'

The training routine for Sea The Stars in advance of the Derby was not materially altered to ensure that he lasted the longer distance. 'He had worked pretty hard for the Guineas,' declares Oxx, 'so it was nice to have a five-week interval before the Derby. We kept to the same sort of routine, though I might once have worked him for a furlong further.'

With two weeks to go, Sea The Stars was vying for Derby favouritism at around 3-1 with Aidan O'Brien-trained Fame And Glory, an unbeaten colt who had won the Ballysax Stakes and Derrinstown Stud Derby Trial at Leopardstown – the route to Epsom trod by Sea The Stars' half-brother Galileo in 2001 as well as 2002 Derby winner High Chaparral. But on 27 May the Racing Post reported Oxx as having serious doubts about *whether his charge would run at Epsom if the going were soft. The chances at that point, said the trainer, were 50-50: 'If there was a wet week leading up to the race and plenty of cut, I would seriously consider not running him.'*

But all was well. The feared rain did not fall in sufficient quantity to jeopardise the chances of Sea The Stars following in the hoofprints of Nashwan, twenty years earlier the last horse to win both the 2,000 Guineas and the Derby, and on 6 June he walked into the paddock to face 11 rivals for the first running of the 'Blue Riband of the Turf' under the sponsorship of Investec, the specialist bank.

To be accurate, when Sea The Stars was walking calmly round the Epsom paddock he was in the company of only five rivals, as the six-strong Aidan O'Brien team arrived so late for their exposure to public scrutiny that the trainer was fined by the Epsom stewards, who were reported to have taken 'a dim view' of their tardiness.

With half the field from one stable and two-thirds of the runners trained in Ireland, the line-up for England's most historic race had a lopsided look.

In addition to the warmly fancied Fame And Glory, ridden by Seamie Heffernan, the O'Brien squad consisted of Rip Van Winkle, who had not run since finishing fourth behind Sea The Stars at Newmarket and remained the choice of stable jockey Johnny Murtagh; Black Bear Island, two places ahead of Sea The Stars in that Curragh maiden race eleven months earlier and most recently winner of the Dante Stakes at York; Golden Sword, surprise winner of the Chester Vase the previous month; Masterofthehorse, third to Sea The Stars in the 2008 Beresford Stakes and runner-up to Golden Sword at Chester under a controversial ride by Murtagh, who had left the horse with an enormous amount of ground to make up in the straight; and Age Of Aquarius, winner of the Lingfield Derby Trial.

Another well-supported Irish challenger was Jim Bolger-trained Gan Amhras, who had not run since coming third in the 2,000 Guineas.

Facing the Irish was a very unprepossessing home team. Brian Meehan-trained Crowded House, spectacular winner of the 2008 Racing Post Trophy, had been desperately disappointing in the Dante Stakes. The Godolphin colt Kite Wood attracted some each-way support, not least because Frankie Dettori was in the saddle, while Debussy (winner of the Blue Riband Trial Stakes over the last ten furlongs of the Derby course before finishing third in the Chester Vase) and rank outsider Montaff completed the field.

Epsom punters seeking a short cut round the intricacies of the form book and Sea The Stars' pedigree would have been advised to take a detour to the Amato Inn on Chalk Lane on their way up to the Downs. Tradition decrees that, over the weekend before the big race, under cloak of darkness a lone gipsy chalks up the name of the Derby winner on the wishing well outside the pub, and although the mystery Romany had not got it right since tipping Galileo in 2001, on the Monday morning before the 2009 race Joe Keeling, owner of the Amato Inn, went outside and saw the name duly chalked up: SEA THE STARS. 'I back the named horse every year and I could do with a winner,' said Keeling before the Derby, 'so I hope Sea The Stars does the business.'

Doubts about the Oxx colt's stamina niggled at the betting public, who sent off Fame And Glory – twice winner over ten furlongs at Leopardstown earlier in the season – the 9-4 favourite, with Sea The Stars on 11-4, Rip Van Winkle 6-1, Black Bear Island 7-1 and Gan Amhras 8-1. Crowded House on 20-1 was the shortest-priced English-trained runner.

Again it was Jon Lees who filed the main race report for the Racing Post, *and again he was reaching for the superlatives …*

The wishing well at the Amato Inn before the 2009 Derby.

Unflappable Sea The Stars breezes to historic win

JON LEES

7 June 2009

THERE have been many memorable Derby winners in between but, like Nashwan in 1989, Sea The Stars proved he belonged in another galaxy by completing the 2,000 Guineas–Derby double yesterday.

By such feats is greatness measured, and Sea The Stars sealed his place alongside Sir Ivor, Nijinsky and Nashwan with a sublime victory at Epsom.

Given a '50-50' chance of staying the Derby distance by his trainer John Oxx before the Classic, he was ridden with maximum confidence by veteran jockey Mick Kinane who, two weeks short of his 50th birthday, clinched the Investec-sponsored prize for 27-year-old Hong Kong businessman Christopher Tsui.

They led home an Irish one-two-three-four-five as horses trained by Aidan O'Brien, who saddled half the field of 12, filled the next four placings, with 9-4 favourite Fame And Glory – the subject of a late plunge that displaced Sea The Stars at the head of the market – finishing second from Masterofthehorse, Rip Van Winkle and Golden Sword.

Nothing bothered Sea The Stars yesterday as the colt, perhaps having inherited his trainer's unflappability, breezed through the preliminaries and the race.

Kinane had him settled on the rail in fourth place at the head of the group chasing the pacesetting Golden Sword and

Opposite: Before the Derby. Above, top-hatted Aidan O'Brien briefs his six jockeys. Below, the jockeys' photo-call: back row: Frankie Dettori, Jamie Spencer, Jimmy Fortune; middle row: Pat Smullen, Colm O'Donoghue, Johnny Murtagh, Richard Hughes; front row: Richard Hills, Mick Kinane, Seamie Heffernan, Ryan Moore, Kevin Manning. The black armbands are marking the death of trainer Vincent O'Brien, who died earlier that week.

Opposite: Tattenham Corner. Golden Sword leads from Age Of Aquarius, followed by Kite Wood in the Godolphin blue and Sea The Stars on the rail, with Fame And Glory to his outside.

GARY WITHEFORD
horseman

'On Derby Day I went across to the start to help put Sea The Stars into the stalls. As I walked him down that last hundred yards towards the start there was a lot of hustle and bustle, with people on the rails on each side of the course, but he just walked placidly down. Everything else in the field was beginning to get stirred up yet he remained as calm as ever, looking from side to side into everybody's eyes as he walked down. After I'd put him in I rode back to the stands in the starter's car, and coming round Tattenham Corner and seeing that Sea The Stars had won the Derby was the greatest feeling in my life – the greatest feeling ever.'

Age Of Aquarius, and he was travelling ominously well when he began to make a move forward three furlongs out.

Heading Golden Sword at the furlong pole, Sea The Stars galloped into the clear and, encouraged by Kinane, stretched to a length-and-three-quarter win over Fame And Glory, who edged out his stablemates in a photo for the placings.

Kinane had ridden Sea The Stars' half-brother Galileo to Derby success in 2001 and yesterday completed his tenth victory in a British Classic.

'Every step of the way I was winning today,' he said. 'I was a little worried he was over-racing a bit because he just found the pace too slow. It was special to go out there when you ride a favourite and class comes into play. It doesn't happen very often. The last time was when I rode his half-brother.

'He has a very high cruising gear. He had improved enormously from Newmarket – we had to chase him hard to get there.

'Only a horse of his constitution would have taken what we threw at him, but since then it's been a coast.

'He hit the gates on fire and I thought I was going to have to lead or sit behind the leader. I decided to take him back to where I was comfortable and then I got to a position where I was eight lengths down.

'I was able to ride my horse to get there going to the furlong marker. It was never in any doubt. I didn't think anything was going to beat me coming from behind. This horse has given me a new lease of life.'

Victory put Sea The Stars in line for a shot at the Triple Crown – the Classic treble of 2,000 Guineas, Derby and St Leger – but both Oxx and Kinane were lukewarm about the challenge as an option for the colt.

'I think that might be a bridge too far,' said Oxx. 'I'm a believer in the Triple Crown. I think it will be won and probably within the next ten years with the very good stallions that are about that get horses to stay. We were

JOHN OXX

'When he got down off him in the winner's enclosure after the Derby, Mick just whispered to me, "This is one of the greats." He didn't say it to anyone else, because you just couldn't say it then. It wasn't enough to have won the Guineas and the Derby; he had to go on and win the rest. Mick is always very careful, and when he said "This is one of the greats" it was a very significant statement. We kept it to ourselves, as you can't just say it: you have to prove it.'

worried going into the Derby, and we'd be very worried going into the Leger if we had him entered.

'If I said it to Michael he'd be worried we were finally losing our marbles. If we make an entry for the St Leger it might be just a mischievous entry.'

Races over 1m2f are more likely targets, with the Coral-Eclipse, for which the sponsors introduced Sea The Stars as 5-4 favourite, among those that will be seriously considered.

Oxx said: 'We will look at the Irish Derby but he has to have good, fast ground. It hasn't stopped raining in Ireland for about two and a half years. We'll see what it's like at the Curragh but he wouldn't run if it was soft and the Eclipse the following Saturday would be an obvious alternative.

'With the Arc, again the weather is an issue. The big mile-and-a-quarter races would be just up his street, the Eclipse maybe, the International, Irish Champion and Champion Stakes at Newmarket are the obvious races for him.'

He added: 'This horse has a magnificent presence. He was a beautiful yearling. He did everything right. He took no breaking. Right from the word go everything was right. He has never let us down. He's gone right to the very top of the ladder.

'I was not very anxious at any time during the race because he was going so well. He had a lovely position, he cruised down the hill and I could see Mick was waiting, waiting, waiting to pick up the pacemaker. When he sent him on I knew he wouldn't stop. He was going too well for too long.'

Sea The Stars goes past Golden Sword into the lead, as Fame And Glory (no. 5) and Rip Van Winkle (no. 11) go in vain pursuit.

This was most definitely a Derby of real note, won by a colt of the highest class

ALASTAIR DOWN
7 June 2009

NEITHER accident nor statistical freakery dictate that colts who can win a Guineas and a Derby are treasured rarities; they come along with the frequency of Halley's Comet simply because the defining asset of genuine speed is an uneasy bedfellow with the virtue of real stamina.

But yesterday at an overcast Epsom, Sea The Stars elevated himself into the upper echelon of the modern era when travelling with supreme ease throughout to win the Derby almost untroubled. What made you do a double take was not some massive winning margin but the fact that, off an inexplicably funereal early gallop, at no stage whatsoever did Sea The Stars look like getting beat.

With six Ballydoyle runners and an oft-expressed stamina doubt about Sea The Stars, we had all expected that at least one of the O'Brien runners would go a right rattle in order to draw the teeth from their principal target horse. But Golden Sword and Age Of Aquarius just lolloped along in front like a couple of boys in no hurry to reach the school gates of a morning. It was a baffling

Opposite: Coming into the winner's enclosure, where (above) Christopher Tsui follows and (below) Urban Sea's trainer Jean Lesbordes (grey top hat) pays his respects to her second Derby-winning son.

failure to seize the tactical initiative by Ballydoyle and impose their own blueprint on the race.

Although Sea The Stars took a furlong or so to settle and tone down into the lack of pace, Mick Kinane – as unflappable a pair of old eyebrows as ever peered down the gunsight of a horse's ears – was never anywhere else than exactly where he wanted to be. It is not often you see a horse in a Derby patently in need of the field going half a yard quicker, but that is how far into his comfort zone the winner was from flagfall.

John Oxx, admirable trainer and most solid of men, will get plenty of plaudits for this triumph, but I suspect his real skill lay in shoehorning a Guineas preparation into the colt after he had met with a setback. Kinane, all complementary understatement to Oxx's unflashy approach, said that they had 'to chase Sea The Stars into the Guineas' and that it had been a 'coast' to Epsom.

Having to turn up the heat on a Guineas colt is always tricky, but here Oxx was helped by this horse's wonderful temperament. He said: 'This horse is a big, strong masculine presence in the yard. He knows he is boss but is trouble-free and in the same mental form every day. There is anxiety and a weight of responsibility with a horse like him but he makes it a lot easier.' Kinane is also a huge fan of the horse as an individual and, the other day, vouchsafed to a friend of his: 'When I walk this horse on to the Curragh he counts every sheep he passes and I swear he could tell you if one was missing!' As for Oxx, while he doubtless has his occasional human moments, there is something profoundly unflappable and straightforward about the man.

He trains from his father's old stables on the very edge of the Curragh and there is a permanence about the place, an air of solidity.

My feeling is that we may not see a great deal of Sea The Stars over a mile and half in future. He has ticked the

JOHN LYNES

groom (opposite)

'When he won the Derby it was an unbelievable feeling. I'd led up Alamshar when he won the Irish Derby at the Curragh and never thought I'd get to look after another one like him: I certainly never thought I'd get a winner of the Derby at Epsom. Everything on Derby day happened so quickly, and it wasn't until a few days later that it really started to sink in.'

stamina box by passing Signor Tesio's famous piece of wood in the Derby, but is loaded with speed and has that awesomely easy way of going about that marks him as exceptional.

In purely commercial terms the great ten-furlong races are the ones that send the tills into hyperdrive but, more importantly, they look to be exactly where Sea The Stars will shine brightest and play most to his strengths.

The more you watch yesterday's Derby, the more unarguable Sea The Stars' superiority becomes. Kinane hardly had to go after him and only in the last 200 yards did he pick up his whip and give three far from ferocious smacks, like a man thinking, 'This is the Derby, so I better just give him a half-hearted one for the sake of appearances'.

The pundits and analysts will now go to work on quantifying the merit of this win as that is their job.

Comparisons with Nashwan, the last to land this hen's teeth double, are inevitable. But the exact maths does not matter. What is important is that this was a result we can all be happy with, in that we have a colt who has notched a benchmark achievement and fed our unquenchable appetite for a star.

Owner Christopher Tsui is a Hong Kong businessman whose interests are said to include a night club and whose mother Ling bred Sea The Stars from her Arc winner Urban Sea and wasn't standing at the back of the queue when it came to handing out the brains to plan successful matings for her star mare.

I am not sure Oxx is a man likely to kick over the traces by suddenly starting to take clubbing holidays in Hong Kong – John's ecstasy will continue to come on afternoons such as the one Sea The Stars provided yesterday. As for the 49-year-old Kinane, when he turns up the bouncers on the doubtless very upmarket door will politely suggest, 'You come back and pick the kids up later, sir.'

This was most definitely a Derby of real note, won by a colt of the highest class and trained by a man of wisdom, manners and calibre.

What is exciting is not just that Sea The Stars has won a Guineas and a Derby, but that he has taken both with plenty in reserve. That means, God willing, there will be more days when we can sample his magnificence.

ANALYSIS

Graham Dench

There had not been a smaller Derby field since Nijinsky won in 1970, but it was a quality line-up nevertheless, with no complete no-hopers, and it looked relatively open, too, as the betting confirmed, with bookmakers going 7-2 the field and having five runners at single-figure odds in the morning. The make-up was quite extraordinary, however, with none of the four home-trained runners trading at shorter than 20-1 and the remainder of the runners all hailing from Ireland, and all six of them credible contenders in their own right.

Irish-trained runners took the first five places, with the impressive 2,000 Guineas winner SEA THE STARS confirming himself a colt of the very highest class by completing a double last achieved by the great Nashwan 20 years previously and leading home four O'Brien-trained runners, who passed the post almost in line abreast.

The Guineas form was very strongly represented, with Sea The Stars joined by third-placed Gan Amhras and fourth-placed Rip Van Winkle. So, too, were most of the main trials, with Derrinstown winner Fame And Glory treading the route taken in successive years by High Chaparral, Galileo and Sinndar; his stablemates Golden Sword and Masterofthehorse following the Chester Vase path last taken successfully by Quest For Fame; Black Bear Island, another from the same stable, coming on here from the Dante, as had North Light, Motivator and Authorized; and Age Of Aquarius, yet another from Ballydoyle, representing the Lingfield Trial which last produced a Derby winner in High-Rise in 1998. The Racing Post Trophy, which has been such a strong guide in recent years, was also represented, by its winner Crowded House.

Sea The Stars had his stamina to prove, like all Guineas winners, but while his sire Cape Cross gave cause for some concern, the dam Urban Sea had won the Arc and had already produced a Derby winner in Galileo, so he was a far more likely stayer than most of the eight who had tried and failed since Nashwan.

In the event, Sea The Stars' stamina was not fully tested, for the O'Brien front-runners Golden Sword and Age Of Aquarius looked to go very steady for the first two furlongs and then dictated a pace that appeared to be designed to aid suspect stayer Rip Van Winkle rather than Fame And Glory, whose best chance of beating the eventual winner was for stamina rather than for speed yet surprisingly took up a position behind him.

Unlike some, Sea The Stars was thoroughly composed and relaxed throughout the preliminaries, but he raced quite keen to begin with. Once the pace picked up he travelled like a dream, disputing third with Kite Wood behind the two clear leaders, and three out he was clearly going best, while his main rivals were all hard at work. As Age Of Aquarius cracked Sea The Stars was sent in pursuit of Golden Sword, and having taken the leader's measure a furlong from home, he was not at all hard pressed, receiving just three cracks of the whip to keep his mind on the job and make sure. The winning margin was not extravagant, but it was another performance of sheer class and one that placed him firmly among the sport´s true greats.

Fame And Glory had beaten the same horses both times in the Ballysax and the Derrinstown, and there remained a doubt about the strength of the form. He acquitted himself extremely well in second, but he could not quicken with Sea The Stars and never looked as if he was going to beat him. A more searching test might have suited him better, but the suspicion was that Sea The Stars would always have his measure over this distance or shorter, provided the ground was suitable. That proved to be the case, but he had his own moment of Classic glory when a wide-margin winner of an Irish Derby.

EPSOM (L-H)
Saturday, June 6

OFFICIAL GOING: Derby course - good (good to firm in places; 8.3) changing to good after race 1 (1.25); 5f course - good to firm (good in places; 8.7)
Wind: Fresh, behind Weather: Showery

2705	INVESTEC DERBY (GROUP 1) (ENTIRE COLTS & FILLIES)	1m 4f 10y

3:45 (3:53) (Class 1) 3-Y-O

£709,625 (£269,000; £134,625; £67,125; £33,625; £16,875) **Stalls** Centre

Form						RPR
11-1	**1**		**Sea The Stars (IRE)**[35] 1675 3-9-0 121 .... MJKinane 4			124+
			(John M Oxx, Ire) *lw: t.k.h early: handy in main gp: 4th st: wnt 3rd 3f out: chsd ldr gng wl 2f out: rdn to ld ent fnl f: in command and pushed out fnl 100yds*		**11/4**[2]	
1-11	**2**	1 3/4	**Fame And Glory**[27] 1910 3-9-0 122 .... JAHeffernan 10			121
			(A P O'Brien, Ire) *w'like: scope: hld up in midfield: 5th st: rdn and hdwy 3f out: sn swtchd rt: chsd ldng pair over 1f out: r.o wl fnl f to go 2nd towards fin: nvr gng to rch wnr*		**9/4**[1]	
30-2	**3**	nk	**Masterofthehorse (IRE)**[30] 1800 3-9-0 111 .... RichardHughes 2			120
			(A P O'Brien, Ire) *swtg: stdd s: hld up in last trio: 10th st: rdn and hdwy wl over 2f out: r.o wl fnl f to go 3rd on post: nvr gng to rch wnr*		**16/1**	
10-4	**4**	nse	**Rip Van Winkle (IRE)**[35] 1675 3-9-0 115 .... JMurtagh 9			120+
			(A P O'Brien, Ire) *swtg: hld up in midfield: rdn and effrt 3f out: edging lft after: swtchd rt over 1f out: stll edging lft but styd on strly fnl f: wnt 4th last stride: nt pce to rch wnr*		**6/1**[3]	
5-41	**5**	shd	**Golden Sword**[30] 1800 3-9-0 109 .... CO'Donoghue 7			120
			(A P O'Brien, Ire) *led at stdy pce for 2f: wnt clr over 9f out: rdn wl over 2f out: hdd ent fnl f: no ex u.p: lost 3 pls towards fin*		**25/1**	
21-0	**6**	6	**Crowded House**[23] 2014 3-9-0 120 .... JamieSpencer 12			110
			(B J Meehan) *stdd after s: hld up in rr: 11th st: rdn and hdwy on outer over 2f out out: edgd lft and hmpd 2f out: no hdwy after*		**20/1**	
4-1	**7**	1/2	**Age Of Aquarius (IRE)**[28] 1872 3-9-0 109 .... PJSmullen 1			109
			(A P O'Brien, Ire) *swtg: chsd ldr: clr of remainder over 8f out: 2nd st: rdn over 2f out: lost 2nd 2f out: wknd u.p over 1f out*		**25/1**	
-113	**8**	nk	**Debussy (IRE)**[30] 1800 3-9-0 103 .... JimmyFortune 5			109
			(J H M Gosden) *t.k.h: hld up in midfield: rdn and effrt on inner 3f out: wknd 2f out*		**33/1**	
11-5	**9**	4 1/2	**Kite Wood (IRE)**[23] 2014 3-9-0 108 .... LDettori 8			104
			(Saeed Bin Suroor) *swtg: t.k.h: chsd clr ldng pair: 3rd and pushed along st: wknd over 2f out: wl btn and eased ins fnl f*		**28/1**	
2-31	**10**	hd	**Black Bear Island (IRE)**[23] 2014 3-9-0 112 .... RyanMoore 3			101
			(A P O'Brien, Ire) *stdd s: t.k.h: hld up in last trio: last st: rdn and sme hdwy 3f out: sn struggling and wl hld fnl 2f*		**7/1**	
2-3	**11**	5	**Gan Amhras (IRE)**[35] 1675 3-9-0 115 .... KJManning 6			93
			(J S Bolger, Ire) *t.k.h: hld up in midfield: rdn 4f out: 9th st: sn drvn and wknd: wl bhd fnl 2f*		**8/1**	
21-2	**12**	11	**Montaff**[28] 1872 3-9-0 106 .... RHills 11			76
			(M R Channon) *swtg: in tch in main gp: 8th and losing pl st: wknd and bhd fr wl over 2f out*		**40/1**	

2m 36.74s (-2.16) **Going Correction** 0.0s/f (Good) **12 Ran** SP% **122.5**
Speed ratings (Par 113): **107,105,105,105,105 101,101,101,98,97 94,87**
toteswinger: 1&2 £2.20, 1&3 £9.80, 2&3 £10.70 CSF £8.80 TOTE £3.40: £1.50, £1.50, £5.00;
EX 11.20 Trifecta £228.30 Pool: £62,008.79 - 200.91 winning units..
Owner Christopher Tsui **Bred** Sunderland Holdings **Trained** Currabeg, Co Kildare

Masterofthehorse, Rip Van Winkle and Golden Sword finished pretty much upsides Fame And Glory. Masterofthehorse had only a couple behind him into the straight, but he enjoyed a trouble-free run through from the back of the field and challenged for second between his stablemates inside the final furlong. This was a cracking effort, but he failed to reproduce the form.

Rip Van Winkle was held up to get the trip and stayed much better than many expected. Indeed he might have been second but for his inclination to edge left down the camber. One could see why connections, and Murtagh in particular, rated him so highly, and their opinion of him was fully vindicated as the season went on.

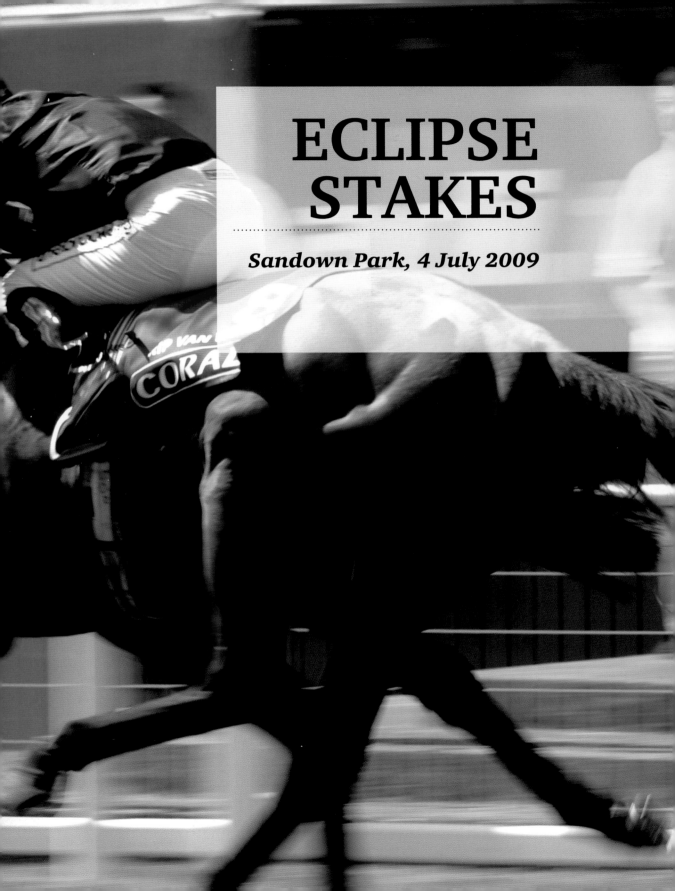

ECLIPSE STAKES

Sandown Park, 4 July 2009

3.15 *Coral-Eclipse (Group 1) (Class 1)* **CH4**
RACE 3 | *Winner £283,850* | (1m 2f 7y)**1m2f**

£500000 guaranteed **For** 3yo+ **Weights** 3yo colts and geldings 8st 10lb; fillies 8st 7lb 4yo + colts and geldings 9st 7lb; fillies 9st 4lb **Weight for age** 3 from 4yo+ + 11lb **Entries** 89 pay £1250 **1st Forfeit** 40 pay £1500 **Confirmed** 14 pay £1250 **Penalty value 1st** £283,850 **2nd** £107,600 **3rd** £53,850 **4th** £26,850 **5th** £13,450 **6th** £6,750

1 (2) 7190-61 **CIMA DE TRIOMPHE** (IRE) [37] [CD]
gr c Galileo-Sopran Londa
L M Cumani Teruya Yoshida — C-P Lemaire — 4 9-7 (126)

2 (9) 12111-2 **CONDUIT** (IRE) [37] [D]
ch c Dalakhani-Well Head
Sir Michael Stoute Ballymacoll Stud — Ryan Moore — 4 9-7 (134)

3 (10) 80206-9 **LANG SHINING** (IRE) [51]
ch h Dr Fong-Dragnet
Sir Michael Stoute Ballymacoll Stud — Richard Hughes — 5 9-7 (117)

4 (1) 2-24378 **STEELE TANGO** (USA) [14] [C]
ch c Okawango-Waltzing Around
R A Teal The Thirty Acre Racing Partnership — Darryll Holland — 4 9-7 (120)

5 (8) 172-334 **TWICE OVER** [17] [D]
b c Observatory-Double Crossed
H R A Cecil K Abdulla — T P Queally — 4 9-7 (129)

6 (3) 14312-7 **JUKEBOX JURY** (IRE) [12]
gr c Montjeu-Mare Aux Fees
M Johnston A D Spence — Royston ffrench — 3 8-10 (121)

7 (4) 1-30 **MALIBU BAY** (USA) [27]
b c El Prado-Favorite Funtime
A P O'Brien (IRE) Mrs John Magnier, M Tabor & D Smith — C O'Donoghue — 3 8-10 (106)

8 (6) 117-44 **RIP VAN WINKLE** (IRE) [28]
b c Galileo-Looking Back
A P O'Brien (IRE) Mrs John Magnier, M Tabor & D Smith — Jimmy Fortune — 3 8-10 (128)

9 (5) 411-11 **SEA THE STARS** (IRE) [28]
b c Cape Cross-Urban Sea
John M Oxx (IRE) Christopher Tsui — M J Kinane — 3 8-10 (134)

10 (7) 184-400 **SET SAIL** (IRE) [18]
ch c Danehill Dancer-Ahdaab
A P O'Brien (IRE) D Smith, Mrs J Magnier, M Tabor — J A Heffernan — 3 8-10 (115)

2008 (8 ran) Mount Nelson (1) A P O'Brien 4 9-7 7/2 | J Murtagh RPR123

BETTING FORECAST: 4-6 Sea The Stars, 7-2 Conduit, Rip Van Winkle, 9 Cima de Triomphe, 16 Twice Over, 66 Jukebox Jury, 100 Steele Tango, 200 bar.

Previous spread: Sea The Stars goes clear.

Winning the Derby as well as the 2,000 Guineas made Sea The Stars a stallion prospect to drool over, with a valuation of as much as £40m widely bandied about. Leading bloodstock agent Charlie Gordon-Watson did a quick sum for the Racing Post: 'Conservatively, he is going to stud with a covering fee of €100,000. With 150 mares that would be €15m – €45m over three years – with additional dual hemisphere value, so £40m is not optimistic. He is a half brother to the most prolific stallion of the moment in Galileo, and that is a big plus. He has speed over a mile and stamina for a mile and a half, although a mile and a quarter looks like being his perfect distance. He is very versatile, is well conformed and has every attribute one wants.'

But Sea The Stars' stallion career lay in the future, and the Tsuis declared that no arrangement about where he would stand at stud would be made until his racing career was over. Meanwhile there were more races to be run. The natural post-Derby target was the Dubai Duty Free Irish Derby at the Curragh – practically in Sea The Stars' back yard – on Sunday 28 June, and as he had come through his Epsom exertions in very good order his training regime was now geared towards the premier Irish Classic, run 22 days after the English equivalent. 'I kept him in the same routine, as he was happy and enjoying himself and eating up,' John Oxx remembers. I didn't give him a week's trotting along the way because he's happier on the move.'

By now Sea The Stars' connections were adamant that they would not run him in unfavourably soft going, but as Irish Derby weekend approached things seemed on course. Then on the Thursday, three days before the race, the weather forecast predicted that the Curragh would be hit by significant rain that evening and on the Friday. Oxx announced that Sea The Stars – who had been a warm odds-on favourite before weather prognostications started to ease his price – would be declared on the Friday, but the final decision might be left to the morning of the race. He added that were Sea The Stars to miss the Irish

Derby, the colt would be redirected to the Coral-Eclipse Stakes at Sandown Park the following Saturday.

Sure enough, the rains came, the Curragh going for the Saturday card was declared 'good to yielding', and to no one's surprise it was announced that Sea The Stars would miss the Irish Derby and head for Sandown. Mick Kinane – who had turned 50 six days before the Irish Derby – put the blame for Sea The Stars' non-appearance squarely at the feet of the racecourse executive: 'The Curragh has only itself to blame for his absence. They over-watered, although there was always the chance of rain.'

Early in Eclipse week John Oxx extinguished the faint hope that Sea The Stars might be trained for the St Leger and bid to become the first Triple Crown winner since Nijinsky in 1970, and with that loose end tied up, attention switched to Sandown Park.

The Eclipse Stakes has long enjoyed a special place in the racing calendar as the first occasion on which top-class middle-distance three-year-olds take on their elders, thereby delivering the first serious comparison of the generations. Plenty of Derby winners have gone on from Epsom to Sandown, and many a reputation has been dented – sometimes irreparably – on the Esher slopes. Since Nashwan completed the Derby-Eclipse double in 1989 (having also won the 2,000 Guineas), four Derby winners had been beaten at Sandown: Erhaab (1994), Benny The Dip (1997), Motivator (2005) and Authorized (2007). Sea The Stars did not have recent history on his side.

A deluge on the Thursday threatened another swerve – John Oxx had made no bones about it: the horse would not run on going worse than good – but all was well, and on the day Sea The Stars faced nine opponents. Four of these were, like him, three-year-olds, and one was an old rival in the shape of Rip Van Winkle, fourth in both the 2,000 Guineas and Derby: with Johnny Murtagh sitting out a suspension, Jimmy Fortune came in for a gilt-edged spare ride. The other three-year-olds were Set Sail and Malibu Bay, both apparently pacemakers for Rip Van

*Mick Kinane and John Oxx: pre-race
tension in the Sandown Park parade ring.*

*Winkle in what was expected to be a tactically intriguing race,
and Mark Johnston-trained Jukebox Jury, winner of the 2008
Royal Lodge Stakes.*

*The five three-year-olds faced the same number of older
horses, headed by Conduit, who in 2008 had given Sir Michael
Stoute the first St Leger victory of his long and distinguished
career before winning the Breeders' Cup Turf at Santa Anita.
Conduit had started his 2009 campaign when narrowly beaten
by Cima de Triomphe in the Brigadier Gerard Stakes over the
same course and distance as the Eclipse at the end of May. Cima
de Triomphe reopposed in the Eclipse, but Conduit was deemed
likely to turn the tables – though whether he would get within
striking distance of Sea The Stars was quite another matter.
Lang Shining, at five the oldest runner in the field, was to serve
as Conduit's pacemaker; Twice Over, trained by Henry Cecil,
had run a close-up fourth in the Prince of Wales's Stakes at
Royal Ascot; and Steele Tango, fourth behind Tartan Bearer over
course and distance in late April, seemed outclassed.*

*With Sea The Stars (who started 4-7 favourite) and Rip Van
Winkle (11-2) heading the three-year-olds and Conduit (9-2)
and Cima de Triomphe (11-1) at the vanguard of the older
generation, a thrilling Eclipse was in prospect.*

Sea The Stars confirms his place among the greats

JON LEES

5 July 2009

AS if becoming the first horse in 20 years to win the 2,000 Guineas and Derby wasn't enough, Sea The Stars took a step towards equine immortality yesterday.

With the exploits of the great Nashwan as his template, Sea The Stars matched his feat, claiming the Coral-Eclipse Stakes to become only the fifth horse in history to win the Group 1 race and those two Classics in the same season.

There wasn't a patch of green to be seen on the lawns surrounding the winner's enclosure after the race, as a vocal gathering paid tribute to a moment that some had waited two decades to witness.

Sea The Stars, whose owner Christopher Tsui fainted after the race, may not have been as spectacular as Nashwan, a five-length winner of the race in 1989, but he proved no less dominant as he saw off the threat of Rip Van Winkle and Conduit with a bit to spare.

Mick Kinane's plan to sit behind his main foes and deliver his challenge with a furlong to run, as he had done at Epsom, was abandoned from the moment the stalls opened, as Sea The Stars broke too well and had to be settled ahead of the horses he had hoped to track.

Yet the 50-year-old veteran didn't lack confidence in his mount and, although forced to make a forward move at the two-furlong pole, which gave runner-up Rip Van Winkle a target to

Opposite: *Leaving the paddock.*

103

Going to post.

aim at, one admonishing crack of the whip issued to his idling partner a furlong out produced the desired response from Sea The Stars, who pulled a length clear at the line. Sir Michael Stoute's Conduit could never land a blow, finishing four and a half lengths further back with Cima de Triomphe fourth.

Despite Oxx's faith in the colt, he admitted he had had pre-race concerns that there would be a big threat to his superstar.

'I knew there was a good run in Rip Van Winkle,' said Oxx. 'Aidan and Johnny [Murtagh] have been sweet on him all season and I was wondering whether today would be his day.

'The race didn't quite go according to plan, he hit the gates so fast, but he always travels easily. There weren't enough of the good horses in front of him, he was the first of the main contenders, and he ended up in front too long and too early, which wasn't Mick's intention.

'I knew something was going to come at him, but I was impressed with the way he stretched. When he was tackled, he went on again and seemed to finish full of running. This fellow will never win by more than two lengths, he just does enough. Although I admit his enough is more than good enough for me.'

Nashwan went on to win the King George VI and Queen Elizabeth Stakes but, although the race will be considered, Oxx would only confirm the Irish Champion Stakes as an intended target, while appearing to rule out the Prix de l'Arc de Triomphe for which he was cut to 2-1 (from 3) by Totesport.

'The Irish Champion Stakes would be a major objective for him, but we'd have to think about running him again before that.

'The King George is in three weeks and the Juddmonte International is three weeks after that. The horse will have a big say and we'll see how he comes out of this. I can't see him running in two races, so we'll have to give one of them a miss.

'The only real mile and a half race for him is the King George, and that is coming plenty quick enough. We are not seriously considering the Arc for him, although he is entered.

'We would have to miss some of the summer races in order to keep him fresh for the Arc, and there might not be a lot of point in that, as four times out of five the race is run on soft ground, which would not suit.

'We're thinking of Leopardstown and then, maybe, the Champion Stakes at Newmarket would be on the agenda.'

JEFF HOULIHAN
travelling head lad
'For me the stand-out memory was Sandown. When Rip Van Winkle came upsides him and then headed him, he showed his true courage. It was as if he was saying, "Sorry – I'm off," and off he went. And it was the first time we experienced how brilliant the crowd were about him. To have a horse like that was just fantastic.'

Overleaf: *'Sorry – I'm off.'*

Superstar colt proves coolness personified to complete historic treble

ALASTAIR DOWN
5 July 2009

FOR just a few strides a furlong from home the issue of Sea The Stars' immortality suddenly hung in the balance as Rip Van Winkle got upsides in his quest to deny the favourite his historic Guineas, Derby and Eclipse treble.

But the cries of the doubters died in their throats as Mick Kinane asked Sea The Stars to dig in. At Newmarket and then at Epsom we had seen the colt travel, now we saw him get his hands a bit dirty as he answered the call almost instantly to put Rip Van Winkle back to sleep.

Sea The Stars may be famed for his almost ludicrously laid-back nature but there was something almost vicious about the way he slapped Rip Van Winkle aside, not with contempt but with a distinct 'don't even think about it' air.

I am all for pure class in the racehorse but for me it is never the whole story without a spot of blood, sweat and sinew thrown in to show that truly exceptional horses have to have the attitude that goes with the ability.

As we waited for the principals to return to unsaddle, one of the game's best judges walked past with the words 'two very good colts', but for once he was wrong. Rip Van Winkle is

SLIM O'NEILL
assistant trainer

'It was at Sandown that I started to realise that Sea The Stars was something very special. We got clapped into the parade ring and down the walkway to the course, where they were five deep trying to get a good look at him. I'd never experienced anything like that before. People were really taking this horse to their hearts, and that gave me a lump in the throat.'

The winner's enclosure, with Jean Lesbordes again in attendance.

a very good colt, but Sea The Stars is cut from a far richer bolt of cloth – the official margin of separation here was a length, but in fact it was a gulf.

Sea The Stars is piling better on top of the already brilliant. In the Guineas he moved throughout that Rowley Mile with an all-consuming ease and won with at least a couple of bullets left in the chamber.

On Derby Day he seemed to be marching to a drum that was beating in his head alone. Amid the high tension of that watch-spring occasion and trained to the minute, he was to be seen standing at the start resting a leg, for all the world as unflustered and as at ease as a pub regular nursing the second half of his pint at the bar of his local.

And while the massed bands of Ballydoyle did their damnedest to close him down towards the end of that mile and a half, the overwhelming impression formed while watching Sea The Stars throughout the Derby was that at no stage was there a realistic chance of him getting beat.

Yesterday he pulled hard in the first furlong and that is surely a function of the fact that he is loaded with an almost bonkers amount of speed for a proven middle-distance performer. But as soon as Kinane got the message 'no' through to him he was instantly tractable and fully switched off back in fifth.

One of the most warming aspects of watching Sea The Stars is the sheer palpable joy that Kinane clearly derives from riding him and yesterday the old master was tuned to every nuance of a race which for all its small fields has produced some horror stories of jockey miscalculation.

But you don't get to 140, or whatever age Kinane admits to these days, without having antennae tuned finer than a bat's, and he was alive to every very possible scenario of pace change and the floating mines that the pricked balloons of the trailblazers would inevitably become. There is no doubt that youth has its part in the make-up of great riders, but I am not sure vigour is ever a match on the Flat for the priceless asset of long-acquired wisdom and experience.

So much of jockeyship is about the avoidance of error. Yesterday Kinane matched the hour and occasion by doing a professional job in a copybook fashion. Yes, it is what he is paid for, but for sheer consistency I am not sure you can beat him.

Others will quantify Sea The Stars in measures mathematical, but it is the manner of the horse that I find extraordinary. On a genuinely hot afternoon he was coolness itself as he ambled round the paddock beforehand. Nothing particularly unusual in that, but to my eye he didn't look vastly different as he held court in the winner's enclosure afterwards having just completed a treble rare in a sport that goes back centuries.

He just stood there as if he had spent the afternoon doing next to nothing – an astonishing example of coolness while putting others under fire.

It helps when you have a horse like this that he is trained by a man about whom you will not hear a bad word said. John Oxx conducts himself with his flawlessly mannered matter-of-fact approach that is notable for the way he virtually never uses the words 'I' or 'me'. For him it is all about the horse and the team effort that has brought the greatness out of him.

But of course it is that steady hand of Oxx's that orchestrates the symphony of Sea The Stars' brilliance. From day one the colt has seemed exceptional and never has a foot been put wrong with him.

Special events should feel genuinely special. That was the case here. A great horse with a once-in-a-generation temperament, ridden by a master and trained by one of the guys in a white hat. Some day.

Sea The Stars was only the fifth horse ever to win the 2,000 Guineas, Derby and Eclipse Stakes in the same season. The others were:
Flying Fox 1899
Diamond Jubilee 1900
Blue Peter 1939
Nashwan 1989

ANALYSIS

Graham Dench

The Curragh's loss was Sandown's gain and hopes that SEA THE STARS might confirm himself the horse of a lifetime by following further in the footsteps of the great Nashwan over this intermediate trip were gloriously vindicated with yet another performance right out of the very top drawer.

Missing the Irish Derby owing to unsuitable ground gave Sea The Stars the opportunity to match Nashwan's 2,000 Guineas, Derby and Eclipse treble of 1989, and while his winning margin was nowhere near so extravagant as the five lengths by which Nashwan blitzed Opening Verse, Rip Van Winkle was clearly a tougher rival. What's more, the pair left two Classic winners trailing at the end of a race which was run at an end-to-end gallop, thanks to three pacemakers.

The winning time of 2m 3.40s was little more than a second outside subsequent Eclipse winner Kalaglow's course record, which was set in the 1982 Brigadier Gerard Stakes on an afternoon of almost freakishly fast times, and by far the fastest set in the race in more than 40 years, bettering by almost a second the next best achieved by Mtoto in 1987.

Conduit's pacemaker Lang Shining was soon driven to the front, where he proceeded to set a strong pace, closely pursued by Ballydoyle pacemakers Set Sail and Malibu Bay. The principals were all held up at the back of the field, the order barely altering until into the straight, but Sea The Stars was always best placed of them, albeit around 10 lengths off the lead still as they turned in.

At the 3f marker Mick Kinane glanced over his left shoulder and then eased Sea The Stars out for his challenge. With the leaders tiring, having done their job, Sea The Stars made his ground so easily that he was in front 2f out, and that was plenty soon enough here as Rip Van Winkle had followed him through and Conduit was closing too on the wide outside. Both looked dangers around a furlong and a half out, but Sea The Stars soon had only Rip Van Winkle to worry about. His challenge simply spurred him on, for he was firmly on top through the last 150 yards and won yet another major prize without enduring that hard a race.

This was Rip Van Winkle's fourth top-level defeat, but he had been a good fourth in both the 2,000 Guineas and Derby and reports from Ballydoyle were suggesting he was held in as high regard as Mastercraftsman and Fame And Glory. His performance here gave real substance to that claim, for he did enough to be elevated above his two illustrious stablemates on ratings. Subsequent wins in the Sussex Stakes and the Queen Elizabeth II Stakes confirmed beyond doubt that he was a top-class colt in his own right.

We still did not know the full extent of St Leger winner Conduit's ability going into this race, for he had ended 2008 on a steep upward curve and had made a highly encouraging reappearance. He benefited from the sort of pace that had been such a factor in his Breeders' Cup win but he was not quite at his best here. However, just three weeks later he franked this form by beating his stablemate Tartan Bearer in the King George VI and Queen Elizabeth Stakes.

The 2008 Italian Derby winner Cima de Triomphe was not quite good enough to make his mark in domestic Group 1 races, but he had won a Group 3 at Sandown the time before. Steele Tango went on to win a Group 3 at Newmarket in the autumn, while Jukebox Jury, still on the comeback trail, won a Group 1 in Germany. Twice Over, well below par here, went on to win Newmarket's Champion Stakes.

The form could not have worked out better.

SANDOWN (R-H)
Saturday, July 4
OFFICIAL GOING: Good (good to firm places)
Wind: Light, against Weather: Becoming bright, very warm

3640	CORAL-ECLIPSE (GROUP 1)	1m 2f 7y

3:15 (3:17) (Class 1) 3-Y-O+

£283,850 (£107,600; £53,850; £26,850; £13,450; £6,750)　**Stalls** High

Form						RPR
1-11	**1**		**Sea The Stars (IRE)**[28] 2705 3-8-10 124............................. MJKinane 5			135+
			(John M Oxx, Ire) lw: hld up in 5th: smooth prog fr 3f out to ld 2f out: rdn and hrd pressed 1f out: dug deep and fended off chalr last 150yds **4/7**[1]			
0-44	**2**	1	**Rip Van Winkle (IRE)**[28] 2705 3-8-10 119..................... JimmyFortune 6			132
			(A P O'Brien, Ire) hld up towards rr: smooth prog wl over 2f out: wnt 2nd wl over 1f out: potent chal ent fnl f: r.o but hld last 150yds **11/2**[3]			
11-2	**3**	4 ½	**Conduit (IRE)**[37] 2410 4-9-7 125...................................... RyanMoore 9			123
			(Sir Michael Stoute) settled in last: taken to outer and rdn 3f out: prog to go 3rd over 1f out and cl enough: kpt on but outpcd after **9/2**[2]			
0-61	**4**	5	**Cima De Triomphe (IRE)**[37] 2410 4-9-7 116................... C-PLemaire 2			113+
			(L M Cumani) hld up in last trio: effrt whn nt clr run over 2f out: kpt on to take modest 4th jst over 1f out: nvr any ch **11/1**			
4300	**5**	3 ¾	**Steele Tango (USA)**[14] 3139 4-9-7 110..................... DarryllHolland 1			106
			(R A Teal) chsd clr ldng trio: rdn over 3f out: lost pl over 2f out: no ch after: plugged on **100/1**			
12-0	**6**	½	**Jukebox Jury (IRE)**[12] 3230 3-8-10 110..................... RoystonFfrench 3			105
			(M Johnston) settled in midfield: rdn 4f out: effrt u.p and 4th briefly over 1f out: wknd fnl f **50/1**			
-334	**7**	2 ½	**Twice Over**[17] 3013 4-9-7 119... TPQueally 8			102
			(H R A Cecil) lw: hld up in rr: last and nt gng wl over 2f out: plugging on to chal for remote 6th whn hmpd 1f out **14/1**			
30	**8**	11	**Malibu Bay (USA)**[27] 2756 3-8-10 102........................... CO'Donoghue 4			78
			(A P O'Brien, Ire) chsd clr ldng pair tl wknd wl over 2f out **100/1**			
06-0	**9**	6	**Lang Shining (IRE)**[51] 2015 5-9-7 99........................ RichardHughes 10			80
			(Sir Michael Stoute) led after 1f to 2f out: heavily eased over 1f out **150/1**			
-400	**10**	1 ½	**Set Sail (IRE)**[18] 2992 3-8-10 103....................................... JAHeffernan 7			63
			(A P O'Brien, Ire) led 1f: pressed other pcemaker to over 2f out: wknd rapidly **200/1**			

2m 3.40s (-7.10) **Going Correction** -0.15s/f (Firm)
WFA 3 from 4yo+ 11lb　　　　　　　　　　　　**10** Ran　SP% 117.3
Speed ratings (Par 117): **122,121,117,113,110** 110,108,99,94,93
toteswingers: 1&2 £1.90, 1&3 £1.40, 2&3 £3.30 CSF £4.37 CT £8.39 TOTE £1.50: £1.02, £2.10, £1.80; EX 4.20 Trifecta £9.90 Pool: £31,619.58 - 2,346.27 winning units..
Owner Christopher Tsui **Bred** Sunderland Holdings **Trained** Currabeg, Co Kildare

AT HOME

The burning question following the Eclipse was whether Sea The Stars would be aimed at the King George VI and Queen Elizabeth Stakes at Ascot three weeks later. Once widely regarded as the middle-distance championship of the mid-summer, the King George has lost a little of its magnetism in recent years – no Derby winner had run in the race since Kris Kin finished third behind John Oxx-trained Alamshar in 2003 – and an appearance by the dual Classic winner and horse of the moment would have given the race a major fillip.

Oxx had also won the King George in 2005 (when it was run at Newbury as Ascot was building its new stand) with the four-year-old Azamour, and initially it looked possible that Sea The Stars would be aimed at the race. But the three-week interval between Sandown and Ascot was considered too short for a horse being primed for a major autumn campaign which could take in the Juddmonte International Stakes at York in mid-August, the Irish Champion Stakes in early September, and the Prix de l'Arc de Triomphe – now more firmly on the agenda – in early October, and possibly stretching as far as the Breeders' Cup in early November. At some point Sea The Stars would need a break.

'Either I had to keep him going for the King George and miss York,' explains John Oxx, 'or give him a break after the Eclipse, miss the King George and go to York. Mick said to me that if you were designing a racecourse to suit Sea The Stars, you would design York: it was the most perfect course for his way of racing. That was a major factor in deciding to miss Ascot. So for three weeks he didn't do any fast work – he just cantered and put on a little bit of weight.'

Sea The Stars' short break gave Brough Scott the opportunity to go and visit the horse in his home surroundings.

Previous spread: *John Oxx's first lot on the Curragh.*

A pilgrimage to the home of the chosen one

BROUGH SCOTT
19 July 2009

HE'S an idol, not a pet. As Sea The Stars walks through – big, proud, strong and handsome – a strange frisson runs through the John Oxx yard. The people there are too sensible to say it out loud and too busy to spend time gawping, but as the morning progresses the truth becomes obvious. They are not just in charge, they are in awe of their Derby winner. Classic horses do that to you. For they hold out the promise of being 'the chosen one', the reincarnation of all the greatness that has gone before. Being with them makes you part of racing's history.

But sustaining brilliance is more difficult than showing it. Many have threatened to rank among my personal pantheon that numbers Sea Bird, Sir Ivor, Nijinsky, Mill Reef, Brigadier Gerard and Dancing Brave but none, as yet, has truly made it. So when a new contender emerges there is the wish to worship, to hold your breath and above all to make the pilgrimage while the dream still lives.

That's why we were travelling through the mist to the far side of the Curragh on Wednesday. At ten to seven the brightest thing at Currabeg was Alex da Silva's smile. Alex's first experience of anything like a racehorse was in three-and-a-half furlong 'bush races' back home in Northern Brazil. Well, I think that is what he said, but his command of the English language is somewhat less than the cool, feline prowess in the

117

saddle which sees him atop Sea The Stars every morning.

The smile, a wonderful, wide, teeth-flashing, central-casting, coffee-seller of a smile, comes the moment we mention his horse's name. 'Very, Very, Good,' says Alex.

Inside the yard John Oxx is talking to his long-time assistant 'Slim' O'Neill whom John, uniquely, still always addresses as Jimmy. At the racetrack John's public persona is so much that of the quietly spoken, sober-suited, bespectacled, professorial diplomat that it is easy to forget that every morning he and 'Slim' are grafting through all the bumps and pains that make up the daily grind of having 140 volatile, young, equine athletes in your care. John is a spare, purposeful presence in tweed cap, zipped-up body-warmer and gumboots.

Tuesday had been his 59th birthday and he has been here as the official trainer since 1979, and was assisting his father before that. There is no shouting or arm-waving histrionics, but there is no doubt that he is in charge. Especially of that horse over there. Outside Sea The Stars' box there are two brass plaques: one for Alamshar, winner of the 2003 Irish Derby, the other for Sinndar, winner of both that race and the Derby and Arc in 2000 – two real good horses he must now eclipse if he is to be a great one.

Inside the box, John Hynes is calmly clearing the droppings and checking the feet with a long face just as unmoved as it has been in those pictures of him and travelling head lad Jeff Houlihan leading his champion in at Newmarket, Epsom and Sandown. Sea The Stars may have become a Derby winner, but first and always, he remains a horse. And what a horse. At 16'2½ hands (5ft 6½ inches) at the shoulder, 524 kilos on the weighbridge, Sea The Stars cuts a tremendous figure; a truly magnificent, masculine, king of the herd. Here is that perfect mixture of power and poise that every thoroughbred conception aspires too. In purely physical terms he ranks easily amongst the great ones we mentioned – bigger and

ALEX DA SILVA
exercise rider (opposite)
'He walks very slowly and very quietly, very relaxed, but at the gallop he's a machine, with so much power. I speak to him every day: my heart talks to him. He's my friend!'

more stable than Sea Bird, a shade more quality than Sir Ivor, a lot less volatile than Nijinsky, two sizes larger than Mill Reef, easier to handle than Brigadier Gerard, a touch more powerful than Dancing Brave.

The last Guineas winner who looked as good as this was Nashwan. At this stage of the year he had been even more impressive than Sea The Stars and was to top it in the King George, which the new contender will bypass next Saturday. But Nashwan did not last the season. As Oxx is all too well aware. 'People do not know how tough it is to do what this horse has done and will have to do,' he says as we drive slowly across the gorse and grass landscape of the Curragh with Sea The Stars and his stable-companion Mourayan walking beside us. 'Those who complain that Classic horses are wrapped up in cotton wool don't know how hard they are being tested. Sea The Stars started cantering again two weeks after the Beresford [run on September 28 last year] and then cantered six days a week right through the winter. He began his fast work in March, ran a temperature on 17 March, did not get back working until a fortnight that Friday [3 April], got up for the Guineas, had five weeks to the Derby and was in fast work the Tuesday week after Epsom. He may have won the Guineas, the Eclipse and the Derby but he's only halfway through.'

The day before had seen the decision to sidestep the King George for the York International in August and Irish Champion Stakes in September. Beside us, Sea The Stars gives a movement of quick, plunging wellbeing which receives a pat from the phlegmatic da Silva and a rueful reflection from his trainer. 'Maybe we should run in the King George after all,' he says teasingly. 'But York is four weeks on Tuesday. Missing Ascot gives us the chance to ease off a fraction. Then Leopardstown is 18 days after York, the Arc four weeks after that. Of course it could all be sabotaged by the weather. He won't run if it is soft, he won't go to the Far East, but with the new surface we could consider the Breeders' Cup, although

7 November is a long way off. We shall have to play it by ear and see how the horse is.'

The details have such a meticulous, clinical exactitude about them that it is almost a shock to hear the bubbling, uncontained enthusiasm with which Oxx talks of the horse in front of us. 'He was always outstanding from the day he walked into the place,' says Oxx as Sea The Stars and da Silva swoop smoothly past us at the canter. 'He was so easy to break in, did everything we asked, had perfect balance and a great temperament. Then when Mick [Kinane] rode him his first bit of work he said, "This one's the real deal."' Sea The Stars' first ever race, a close and slightly unlucky fourth in a maiden race at the Curragh, had been exactly a year ago on the Saturday. 'We were thrilled with him,' says Oxx. 'For with horses it is not so much what you do as what you don't do. If they have ability they have ability, but with a big horse like him we didn't want to train him hard as a two-year-old. You have to tread a careful path.' This year that path was made more difficult first by the unwanted infection in March and

GRACE CANNIFFE
equine massage therapist
'He's a lovely character, a really fine big horse, with a great physique – just a great athlete. And like all great athletes he didn't have serious problems, but we needed to minimise the smaller problems that crop up. I worked him mainly with my hands, though we have laser and mechanical massage machines as well as ultrasound, and every day it's a case of assessing if there was any new tightness in the muscles and dealing with it. He's been just amazing all year.'

SLIM O'NEILL

assistant trainer (opposite, leading Alex da Silva on Sea The Stars)
'He's a big horse and a little bit of a bully in the stable. Nothing malicious – he'd just push you around a bit. He's strong, and a horse who gets fresh very quick.'

then by a laboured work-out with stablemate Arazan on very soft ground a week before the Guineas. 'The other horse went better than him,' remembers Oxx. 'But, in hindsight, the hard blow probably set him right and it did show us that it would be wrong to ask him to match his present level on soft ground. It also showed us how good was his constitution. I learnt with Sinndar that these real Classic horses need the ability to take a bit more than the others. They need to be really healthy and sound and this horse is all that and a quite exceptional eater.'

Oxx's bright, student son Kevin is in the back of the car just like John used to be with his father John Oxx senior all those years ago. The present trainer is in charge of an extremely expensive, highly competitive, internationally targeted operation.

He deals alike with crowned heads, stable staff and business potentates. But the wellspring of it all walks on four hooves over there. 'I love this,' he says looking across at Sea The Stars profiled against the emerging expanses of County Kildare. 'This is the real pleasure of training racehorses. Most of the time it is a nightmare of a job, but the joy you get is from being around exceptional horses like that, of just watching him walk, of minding him, of seeing him at evening stables, of being able to look at him not just as an athlete but as an individual.'

The significance of that last phrase comes through as Oxx adds: 'This is a big, strong, masculine horse and if you don't work him he gets too fresh. Those two weeks trotting we gave him last year were all we could allow or he would have his rider off. As everyone has seen, he has a terrific big-race temperament, but when he first goes into the racecourse stables he will roar like a stallion. It's a territorial thing. Once he has established who is boss, he's all right.'

Back in the yard the question arises not just of Sea The Stars' schedule but of his future ownership, with racetrack rumours ever swirling of massive bids from Sheikh Mohammed, who already owns the sire Cape Cross, and from

John Magnier, who stands Galileo, the other Derby-winning son of the dam Urban Sea. Oxx opts for no political obfuscation. 'There are people in this world,' he says quietly, 'whose sole motivation is not money. And these people [speaking of the owning Tsui family] are in that category. Which is great for me; the rest of us could not afford not to sell him.

'As regards his stallion career, we can talk about all that later. First we have to remember that he is only halfway through. He has been very good but he hasn't yet done what Sinndar did and he is not yet rated even as high as Alamshar. To be rated up there with them and above, with Nijinksy and Sea Bird, he has to go through to the end of the year, to be tested as the Bible says "like gold in the furnace". But I guess I have to think that he is the best horse that I have ever had.'

The sun has burnt through the mist, and over on the other side of Kildare town the Irish National Stud is welcoming some of the 150,000 visitors who can now add 'birthplace of Sea The Stars' to the place's famous walks, horse museum and unique Japanese Gardens.

'Yes, he was the most wonderful-looking foal,' says chief executive John Clarke. 'Of course you can't remember every foal, but with Urban Sea being an Arc winner herself and being the dam of Galileo, we definitely remember him. He was never sick in his life and had done absolutely everything right by the time he went to John's in the autumn of 2007.'

Clarke has been half a lifetime at the National Stud and stood, tall and elegant, on the winners' podium to receive the trophy on behalf of the Tsui family at Newmarket. His role as representative to owner Christopher Tsui and his remarkable business-tycoon mother Ling Tsui makes him particularly adamant when Sea The Stars' future is discussed. 'The horse,' he says almost sharply, 'is not for sale. I speak to Ling Tsui a lot and everyone is enjoying the fun of an unbelievably good racehorse and I just feel privileged to be part of what is a great adventure for the Tsui family.'

DAVID BOYNE
farrier

'I love sports, and to be involved in a great athlete's career, even playing just a small part in it, is brilliant. Sea The Stars always had good feet, and was never a problem to shoe. When being shod he'd always be so quiet and gentle.'

The feeling of personal involvement has a poignant but playful expression out in the paddock behind us. In March, Urban Sea died suddenly within minutes of foaling a bonny chestnut colt by Invincible Spirit. That night a slightly tubby roan mare called Minipen welcomed the little orphan to her matronly bosom. On Wednesday, the headlines on the Irish papers predicted further economic catastrophe, but out on the grass of Kildare, one little family gave something to lift the spirit.

There was one more visit to be made on this pilgrimage – to the handsome home, 15 miles away near Punchestown, of Sea The Stars' jockey Mick Kinane. On the way there, the logic of the horse's future becomes inescapable. Mrs Tsui, who has the Chinese government as not the least of her international

clients, does not need the money. The Irish National Stud
has both John Oxx as a former chairman and John Clarke as
current chief executive. It is not just Sea The Stars' birthplace
but would be a perfect neutral stallion base for the Tsui family
to relish the delights of vicarious stallion-hood away from the
competing might of Sheikh Mohammed's Darley operation
and John Magnier's Coolmore.

But if that is the horse's destination when will he go there,
and can he really achieve the extra miles on the track to
give him the immortality for which we all yearn? The fittest
50-year-old in racing has been mowing the lawn and that, if
you are Michael Kinane – 34 years, 13 championships and
three Derbys into one of the greatest of all riding careers –

means a lot of lawn to mow. He sits in the state-of-the-art kitchen and ponders the possibilities. 'Honestly,' he says, the lines of the face ageing in emphasis, 'I think this horse can do anything. I just could not believe the ease with which he came up to them in the Eclipse. And as for anything being unlucky in the Derby, that is nonsense. He gets the trip, he has incredible pace. I have been very lucky to have ridden some wonderful horses but I can say this is the best I have ever sat on. I have only seen the likes of Sea Bird, Nijinsky and Mill Reef on the television, but I was around for Dancing Brave. I think this horse is in that bracket.'

It's that feeling of awe again. We are alone in the kitchen but Kinane drops his voice as he describes the thrill of being on board the ace in every rider's pack. But a cloud of doubt comes across the face when we talk about the horse running as a four-year-old. 'I am not privy to anything,' he says. 'But if he were to get through these other races he becomes the most amazing stallion prospect ever. You have to wonder if it's worth the risk.' As we leave, his words produce familiar competing thoughts: disappointment at the possibility of an equine superhero not being tested against a junior generation, and acceptance that one full season can still deliver greatness. None of Sea Bird, Sir Ivor, Nijinsky or Dancing Brave ran as four-year-olds and we don't decry their claim to immortality.

Above all, one day with Sea The Stars and all his County Kildare constellations reaffirms the crucial excitement of what lies ahead. 'We are only halfway through,' Oxx had said on parting, and as we leave Kinane Towers another small, if rather older, figure gets off a mowing machine. It is Tommy Kinane, hero of Monksfield's 1978 Champion Hurdle and self-appointed guardian of his son's estate. 'Ah yes,' he says, eyes wide with enthusiasm when asked about Sea The Stars. 'He's the best, the very best. Mick says he would win the July Cup.'

Not much chance of that now but yes, Tommy is in awe too.

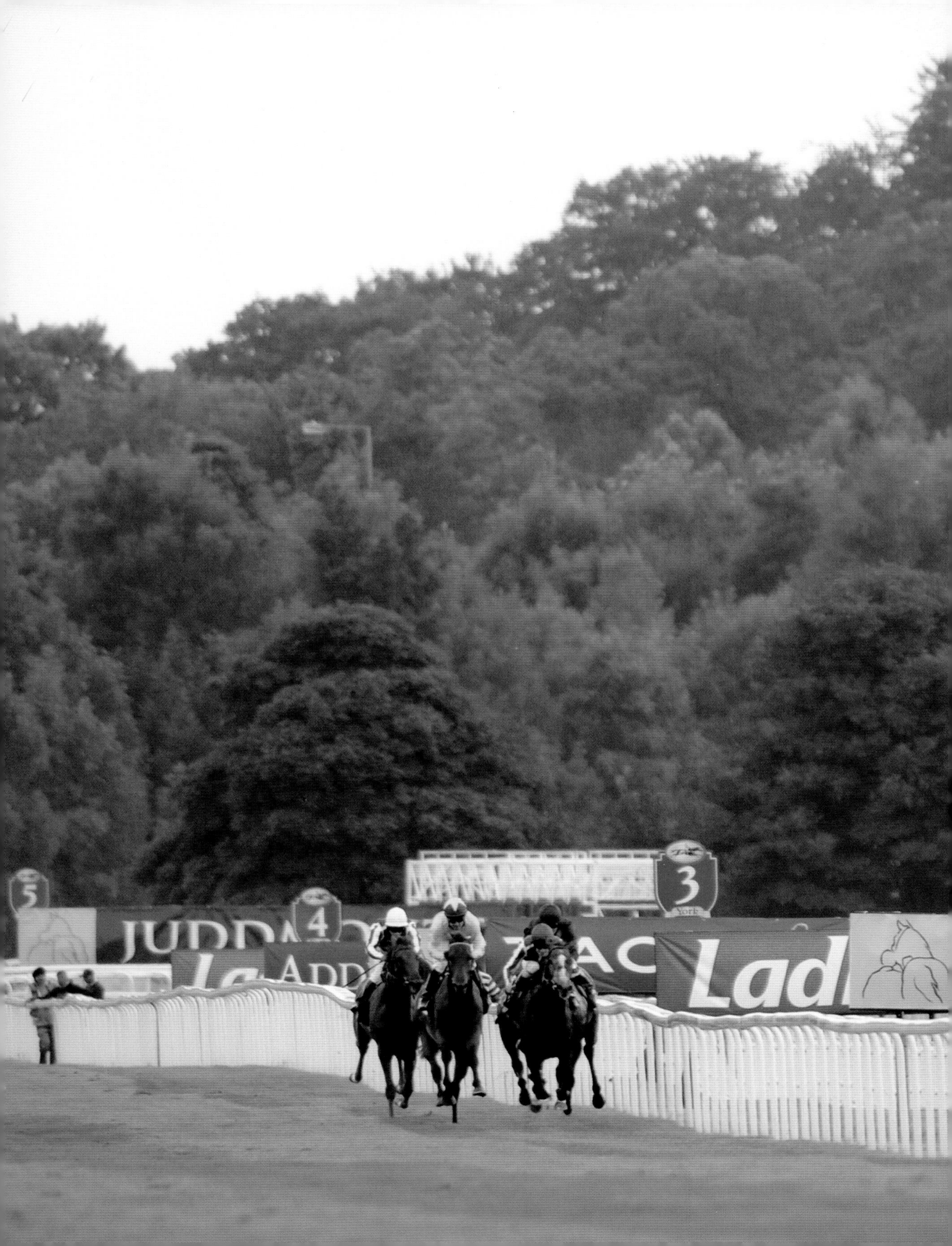
5
JUDD
4
3
Lad

JUDDMONTE INTERNATIONAL STAKES

York, 18 August 2009

3.25 RACE 4	*Juddmonte International Stakes* *(Group 1) (Class 1)* *Winner £340,620*	CH4
		(1m 2f 88y)**1m2½f**

£600000 guaranteed **For** 3yo+ **Weights** 3yo colts and geldings 8st 11lb; fillies 8st 8lb 4yo+ colts and geldings 9st 5lb; fillies 9st 2lb **Weight for age** 3 from 4yo 8lb **Entries** 49 pay £2100 **1st Forfeit** 19 pay £2400 **Confirmed** 8 pay £1500 **Penalty value 1st** £340,620 **2nd** £129,120 **3rd** £64,620 **4th** £32,220

1
(1)
0930233 **GEORGEBERNARDSHAW** (IRE) ¹⁵ [BF]
b c Danehill Dancer-Khamseh
A P O'Brien (IRE) Mrs John Magnier, M Tabor & D Smith
4 9-5
C O'Donoghue (117)

2
(4)
123-122 **TARTAN BEARER** (IRE) ²⁴ [CD]
ch c Spectrum-Highland Gift
Sir Michael Stoute Ballymacoll Stud
4 9-5
NON-RUNNER (134)

3
(2)
114-511 **MASTERCRAFTSMAN** (IRE) ⁶³
gr c Danehill Dancer-Starlight Dreams
A P O'Brien (IRE) D Smith, Mrs J Magnier, M Tabor
3 8-11
J Murtagh (133)

4
(3)
411-111 **SEA THE STARS** (IRE) ⁴⁵ [D]
b c Cape Cross-Urban Sea
John M Oxx (IRE) Christopher Tsui
3 8-11
M J Kinane (143)

5
(5)
4-40002 **SET SAIL** (IRE) ³⁰ [BF]
ch c Danehill Dancer-Ahdaab
A P O'Brien (IRE) D Smith, Mrs J Magnier, M Tabor
3 8-11
J A Heffernan (117)

2008 (9 ran) **Duke Of Marmalade** (4) A P O'Brien 4 9-5 4/6F   J Murtagh RPR128

BETTING FORECAST: 1-3 Sea The Stars, 9-4 Mastercraftsman, 200 Georgebernardshaw, Set Sail.

Previous spread: *Coming up the straight.*

I n 2008 the York August meeting, featuring the historic Ebor Handicap as well as three Group 1 races and a feast of other top-class races over four days, was abandoned in its entirety after torrential rain had made the ground unraceable. So the prime emotion on Tuesday 18 August 2009, opening day of one the Flat season's greatest showpieces, was sheer relief that York's biggest occasion was back in business. The appearance of Sea The Stars in the day's feature event, the Juddmonte International Stakes over ten furlongs, was the icing on the cake.

By this stage of the season it was accepted that the participation of Sea The Stars in any race was subject to ground conditions. He would not run on soft going or worse, and that was that – and alarm bells started clanging when the week before the Juddmonte International the weather forecast predicted a significant level of rain over York. John Oxx confirmed that there was 'a big question mark' over his horse's participation, but the rain failed to materialise, and on the Sunday, two days before the International, Sea The Stars was confirmed a runner.

With the late withdrawal of Sir Michael Stoute-trained Tartan Bearer, runner-up to his stable companion Conduit in the King George VI and Queen Elizabeth Stakes at Ascot, only four runners went to post at York – and if the Derby had had a lopsided look, the profile of this race was even more wonky. Three of the four runners were trained at Ballydoyle by Aidan O'Brien, but only one was a serious threat to Sea The Stars' domination: Mastercraftsman, who since finishing fifth behind our hero in the 2,000 Guineas had won two of the season's most prestigious races for three-year-olds over a mile, the Irish 2,000 Guineas and the St James's Palace Stakes at Royal Ascot. With Sea The Stars going off 1-4 favourite – the shortest starting price he ever returned – Mastercraftsman, ridden by Johnny Murtagh, started at 3-1, with his pacemakers Georgebernardshaw (the only four-year-old of the quartet) and Set Sail priced at 100-1 and 125-1 respectively.

In essence, as James Willoughby stressed in his Racing Post preview on the morning of the race, this was a match …

Stars can write another chapter in York folklore

JAMES WILLOUGHBY
18 August 2009

BACK in the 18th century, York races were held just after the local assizes were completed on the Knavesmire. The assembled gentry were highly entertained by the sight of felons meeting a sticky end on the gallows, but they were rather less enamoured when a similar thing happened to all the good things on the track.

To be fair, York's reputation as a graveyard of favourites is easy to expose as an urban myth with the broad sweep of statistics. People have a disproportionate recall of events that most shock them at the time, and nobody likes to see a sure thing turned over.

Over the next four days of the Ebor festival, which opens today, there doubtless will be a few surprises and perhaps even the odd incomprehensible reverse. But nothing would be retained in the collective memory longer than defeat for Sea The Stars.

The 2,000 Guineas, Derby and Eclipse winner lines up for the Group 1 Juddmonte International in a near match race with Irish 2,000 Guineas and St James's Palace hero Mastercraftsman. The defection of Tartan Bearer makes this the type of scenario that recalls many from the sport's nascent days.

In 1851, for instance, York racecourse staged the so-called 'Match of the Century' over two miles between two winners of the Derby, Voltigeur and The Flying Dutchman. The pair

The star turn arrives.

had met in a similar event the previous year, when The Flying Dutchman's jockey Charles Marlow rode a terrible race after a heavy bout of drinking (lucky for him internet chatrooms did not exist).

This time, however, Marlow exacted revenge with the older horse and was delighted to 'silence the doubters' – an expression still used by some horsemen to this day.

Can the match between Sea The Stars and Mastercraftsman live up to the excitement of its distant forerunner? Well, perhaps it can.

It would be a perverse judge indeed who still doubted the credentials of Sea The Stars, but York's notorious history for witnessing surprise results – however disproportionately they are recalled – is at least something to think about.

Some say that horses can get more on edge here than elsewhere on the lead-up from the racecourse stables, others that the historically lifeless nature of the surface suits some horses more than others. Perhaps the wisest just shake their heads and retort 'randomness, pure randomness' to these fanciful conjectures.

As well as Grundy's defeat in the equivalent race in 1975, it is the reverse suffered by the great Brigadier Gerard three years earlier that most people remember as one of the sport's greatest shocks. The Brigadier was turned over by 12-1 shot Roberto, who had won the Derby but was coming off a miserable performance at the Curragh.

Racing folk have discussed the reason for this surprising outcome with as much fascination as Americans have pondered the shooting of JFK. In both instances, the most likely explanation is the action of a single individual working on his own initiative – Lee Harvey Oswald from the book depository at Dealey Plaza, and jockey Braulio Baeza from the front on Roberto.

If Sea The Stars is to be knocked off this afternoon, it will be partly by the result of a conspiracy strictly in the sporting sense. Mastercraftsman's stablemates Georgebernardshaw and Set Sail presumably will give him a lead until Johnny Murtagh decides it is the right time to strike for home. If Sea The Stars is to be floored, he will have to be outgalloped and outbattled in a race that renders some of his finer athletic gifts redundant.

Make no mistake: ability usually prevails in a horserace, however it is run. But Mastercraftsman will be a tougher nut to crack in a physical encounter than his mercurial stablemate Rip Van Winkle was for Sea The Stars in the Eclipse.

Mastercraftsman is by the speed influence Danehill Dancer. But just like that one's sire Danehill, the Coolmore stallion can get horses who appreciate a test when the dam's side allows it.

Here it may be interesting to recall that the sire of Mastercraftsman's dam Starlight Dreams is the top-class dirt horse Black Tie Affair, who was named US Horse of the Year in 1991 following his victory in the Breeders' Cup Classic over today's trip of 1m2f.

Black Tie Affair was at his best when his jockey made plenty of use of him. Like Mastercraftsman, he had an unusually long stride for his body length and could not quicken like other top horses. We have already seen that his grandson is a similar type, at his best in extremely fast-run races or when conditions place the emphasis on the ability to sustain top speed, rather than increase it.

So it won't be a surprise if the International is a strongly run race. But constructing a particular scenario in which Mastercraftsman could match Sea The Stars may even be doing him a disservice. It is possible that he could be of similar ability to the great horse.

Like the freakishly quick 100m runner Usain Bolt, Mastercraftsman has dimensions expressed in very few of his species who are able to run fast.

Studies in the US have proved that a racehorse's merit is correlated with the length of his stride. Not all long-striding

Sea The Stars in the pre-race parade.

horses are top class and not all top-class horses have a long stride, but the ceiling of a horse's merit is basically a function of how powerfully it can propel itself through the air.

As for Sea The Stars, there is no one particular characteristic of his that stands above the others.

In short, he has it all from speed to stamina, courage to consistency. To see him run is a reminder of what other horses do wrong, even very good ones.

Today's race is going to be something very special, whether Sea The Stars continues his dominance or suffers a similar undoing to Brigadier Gerard and Grundy. Because every one of his races has been special and will be all the more so. For now and forever.

Sea The Stars and Mastercraftsman lock horns.

Shooting for the Stars

DAVID CARR
19 August 2009

DEALING with some 500lb of bomb is one thing, but dealing with half a ton of record-breaking horseflesh is quite another.

While a team of military experts were carrying out a controlled detonation on a massive leftover from the Second World War just up the road in Pickering, the Ballydoyle team got everything right as they tried to defuse the equine explosive that is Sea The Stars. But still they could not quite inflict a first defeat of 2009 on the horse of the year.

Aidan O'Brien fielded all three rivals against the Stanjames.com 2,000 Guineas, Investec Derby and Coral-Eclipse winner as he went for a fourth Group 1 victory in the Juddmonte International, and passing the baton between the trio up front through the 1m2f contest gave the 1-4 favourite much his biggest scare of the season.

True, Sea The Stars looked to be cruising for a stride or two as he moved up under Mick Kinane, after Georgebernardshaw and then Set Sail had set a decent pace to three furlongs out – so much so that a smattering of applause actually broke out in places in the stands as racegoers prepared to welcome something to rival Usain Bolt's display in Berlin.

And like the great Jamaican sprinter, he did break a record – his time of 2min 5.29sec beating the previous course best of 2min 6.09sec set four years earlier by Imperial Stride. But success was far from assured when Kinane took a pull after he made his move between the two pacemakers – who picked up £64,000 and £32,000 for their pains – and at that moment

JOHN OXX
'The way Mick followed Mastercraftsman through the gap was probably a little risky, but making these split-second decisions is what you pay jockeys for.'

141

Johnny Murtagh kicked entering the final quarter-mile on Mastercraftsman, for once getting first run on his old rival.

The Irish 2,000 Guineas winner, who had been more than four lengths adrift in fifth at Newmarket, may have got two lengths up at one point and Kinane had to get serious on the favourite. But Sea The Stars made familiarly relentless progress to lead inside the final 100 yards and was a length clear at the line, the pair drawing a distance clear of the two pacemakers.

'Well done you,' were a generous O'Brien's immediate words of congratulation to winning trainer John Oxx, who admitted he had been concerned for a stride or two.

'I was worried,' he said. 'Two furlongs down I thought, "How far is he going to win?", but then he had to struggle. He had to go through between the two pacemakers and had to take a pull.

'He won handily enough in the end, Mick only gave him a couple of smacks. I think it looked like he was in trouble more than he was. Once Mick picked him up he was very good in a battle and, looking at the re-run, won comfortably enough in the end.

'Mick always says he will never win anything by much more than a length – but as long as he keeps winning we'll be happy.

'Aidan's lads did a good job to set a pace that suited their horse and Mastercrafstman really ran home well.

'Aidan's plan was to run the race to suit Mastercraftsman and he obviously did the right thing because his horse ran the best race of his life.'

Oxx admitted he had left tactics to Kinane – 'When you have Michael Kinane riding for you, you don't have long talks about tactics. What am I going to tell him?', he said – and the veteran rider was relieved his mount proved up to the task.

Kinane said: 'I know Mastercraftsman is tough and they had to ride him to their strengths, so I thought today they would

SLIM O'NEILL
assistant trainer

'At York we walked him all the way across the Knavesmire from the stables to the racecourse early in the morning when it was all pretty quiet, and I rode him round the parade ring a few times, just to familiarise him with place. In fact every time he ran as a three-year-old we'd take him round the ring for a while on the morning of the race.'

take a chance and put the play up to my fellow and make him work. It just took a horse of mine's calibre to beat him.

'The last couple of years have been a search for a good horse and then suddenly a great one comes along in the twilight of my riding life.'

Next month's Tattersalls Millions Irish Champion Stakes beckons, provided the ground is not too soft at Leopardstown, and Sea The Stars is 1-2 favourite with Paddy Power, who quote Fame And Glory at 7-4. Plans are fluid for Mastercraftsman – on whom Murtagh was given a four-day ban (September 1-4) for using the whip with excessive frequency – and O'Brien said: 'I'm not sure what I'll do with him. He's not short of speed, our fellow, and I'd not worry about dropping him back in trip, so he could go back to a mile or stay at a mile and a quarter – we'll have to talk about it.

'It was a great race and there was a moment when it looked as though we might win, but I always knew Mick wasn't going to get into a battle with our fellow too soon and that he would leave his run as late as possible. Our horse loves to be in a battle and he's put up a great performance.

'He's run his heart out and I'm very proud of him, but Sea The Stars is a great horse and has run a great race to beat him.'

Happy crowd pay homage after Stars works hard to stay on top

ALASTAIR DOWN
19 August 2009

WHEN it comes to Sea The Stars' greatest hits yesterday's Juddmonte may not prove the most requested, but that will not have mattered a scrap to those who came to the Knavesmire just so they could say they had clapped eyes on him. And, let's face it, he is worth the shoe leather as there are precious few who can breathe the same rarefied air.

For just a couple of seconds up the York straight the result seemed to hang momentarily in the breeze but that was almost an optical illusion. It came just as Mick Kinane took half a pull on the favourite and Johnny Murtagh flicked up a gear on Mastercraftsman. Then reality and superiority kicked in and, while Sea The Stars had to work for a living, it was only the margin of his superiority rather than the fact of it that was in doubt.

When Kinane talks about this horse his voice and face take on the enthusiasm of a teenager, which he must have been many moons ago, just after the last wolves and wild bears in these islands went on the missing list.

After the race he candidly admitted, 'I probably made it look a little more difficult than it need have been,' but for all the narrowness of the length margin in a race that was only ever going to be tactically complex, there was never a moment when defeat loomed.

145

Though not immune to flights of fancy about racehorses, I have never really bought into the 'look of eagles' school of thought. But somehow Sea The Stars is a sight to behold even when he is just sloping around the paddock.

During the moments before major races there can be real tension in the air and time and again you see horses fall foul of it. But this colt is totally at ease with himself and embedded deep into his own zone of utter comfort. Nothing about the build-up bothers him. I always wondered why they called the period just before the race 'the preamble' until I saw Sea The Stars.

In the race itself he has all the weapons and that means Kinane has every tactical option at his disposal. Freaky sets of circumstances can suddenly conspire against you in any race, but it is hard to imagine a pile of trouble in which Sea The Stars could find himself without being able to extricate himself through sheer raw ability.

John Oxx acknowledged that Kinane's little pull on the horse had made him switch off for a second, but it was the bigger picture rather than the detail that was absorbing the trainer's fine mind. A number of those in the crowd on the Knavesmire had made the journey specifically to see this colt and stand witness to him.

For Oxx that is the privilege that makes each morning a fair one and not an ounce of this colt is lost on his trainer. There is something close to humbling about daily, hands-on association with the great horses, the mucky mornings the building blocks of the marvellous afternoons.

Oxx admits to his 'great pride' in being part of the horse, and there is an ocean of admiration in him for this colt. He, above all others, knows exactly what has been asked of Sea The Stars, can remember the days when the questions at home and then on course suddenly got huge, and how wonderfully emphatic the answers have been.

Of course there is always a downside and you can just see

Oxx getting home, heading straight down the pub, swilling eight pints and getting fighting drunk before being thrown out and barred for being too rowdy. Good job he doesn't have a quadruple Group 1 winner every season or they'd never see him at home.

And while this sport is always about what used to be pounds, shillings and pence, a horse like Sea The Stars ushers other considerations uppermost. He was cheered to the echo as he paraded after his win here and given a right roar into the winner's enclosure.

Minutes later, as he made to leave, the applause was renewed, long and enthusiastic, by as deep a crowd as I have seen packed round the paddock here for the aftermath of a big race.

It was part affection, part respect and very much an expression of human happiness at having been on hand to see a great horse at the peak of his powers. A simple pleasure perhaps, but a profound one for all that.

Sea The Stars is 'given a right roar into the winner's enclosure.'

ANALYSIS

Graham Dench

The defection of the King George runner-up Tartan Bearer was unfortunate and left just four starters, with the 100-1 shot Georgebernardshaw the sole representative of the older generation, but this was nevertheless another race to savour.

The gritty St James's Palace winner Mastercraftsman was widely expected to make SEA THE STARS work if he was to enjoy a fourth successive Group 1 success, but few can have anticipated just how hard he would have to work.

The Ballydoyle pace-setters ensured such a good gallop that the course record was lowered by 0.80 of a second – the equivalent of more than four lengths – but the two principals raced easily behind them, with Mastercraftsman third and Mick Kinane content to wait in last place on Sea The Stars. When Mastercraftsman slipped through a gap between the pacemakers inside the 3f marker Sea The Stars followed him through, with Kinane still motionless and Sea The Stars seemingly set for an easy victory. However, when Mastercraftsman opened up Sea The Stars did not respond immediately, and he further compromised his chance by edging in to the left behind him. He looked in serious trouble, but when Kinane switched him and gave him a couple of smacks with the whip he found plenty, digging deep and running on strongly to lead well inside the final furlong and win going away. Visually it was his least impressive display so far, but it was another top-class performance, and one bettered at this stage only in the Eclipse.

Mastercraftsman had already shown himself to be a top-class miler, and the extra distance had almost certainly brought about further improvement. He was no match in the end for Sea The Stars, but he gave him a fright and stuck on really gamely as the pair went head to head. It was a performance that enhanced his reputation and opened up new possibilities for the remainder of the season.

The pair finished more than 30 lengths clear of the two pacemakers, who could not soften up Sea The Stars quite enough but earned the best part of £100,000 for their trouble.

YORK (L-H)
Tuesday, August 18

OFFICIAL GOING: Good to firm (8.6)
Wind: moderate 1/2 behind Weather: overcast

5135 JUDDMONTE INTERNATIONAL STKS (GROUP 1)   **1m 2f 88y**
3:25 (3:25) (Class 1) 3-Y-O+   **£340,620** (£129,120; £64,620; £32,220)   **Stalls** Low

Form					RPR
-111	**1**		**Sea The Stars (IRE)**[45] 3640 3-8-11 133 .... MJKinane 3		131+
			(John M Oxx, Ire) *lw: hld up in last: hdwy to chse ldr over 3f out: shkn up over 1f out: rdn to ld ins fnl f: r.o*	**1/4**[1]	
-511	**2**	*1*	**Mastercraftsman (IRE)**[63] 2992 3-8-11 122 .... JMurtagh 2		129
			(A P O'Brien, Ire) *swtg: trckd ldrs: smooth hdwy over 3f out: led wl over 2f out: hdd and no ex last 75yds*	**3/1**[2]	
4000	**3**	*32*	**Set Sail (IRE)**[30] 4127 3-8-11 102 .... JAHeffernan 5		65
			(A P O'Brien, Ire) *chsd ldrs: chal over 4f out: wl outpcd over 2f out*	**125/1**	
0302	**4**	*3 1/2*	**Georgebernardshaw (IRE)**[15] 4608 4-9-5 105 .... CO'Donoghue 1		58
			(A P O'Brien, Ire) *led: drvn over 5f out: hdd over 2f out: sn wl outpcd: wknd fnl f*	**100/1**[3]	

2m 5.29s (-7.21) **Going Correction** -0.125s/f (Firm) course record
WFA 3 from 4yo 8lb   **4 Ran**   SP% **106.8**
Speed ratings (Par 117): **123,122,96,93**
 CSF £1.26 TOTE £1.30; EX 1.30.
Owner Christopher Tsui **Bred** Sunderland Holdings **Trained** Currabeg, Co Kildare
■ Stewards' Enquiry : J Murtagh four-day ban: used whip with excessive frequency without allowing mount time to respond (Sep 1-4)

IRISH CHAMPION STAKES

Leopardstown, 5 September 2009

3.50 RACE 5 **Tattersalls Millions Irish Champion Stakes (Group 1)** *Winner €569,000* **CH4** 1m2f

€1000000 guaranteed **For** 3yo+ **Weights** 3yo 9st; 4yo+ 9st 7lb **Weight for age** 3 from 4yo+ 7lb **Allowances** fillies & mares 3lb; southern hemisphere 3yo 5lb **1st Forfeit** 48 **2nd Forfeit** 22 **Confirmed** 11 **Penalty value 1st** €569,000 **2nd** €189,000 **3rd** €89,000 **4th** €29,000 **5th** €19,000 **6th** €9,000

1 (3)
32-2131 **CASUAL CONQUEST** (IRE) [20] CD
b c Hernando-Lady Luck
D K Weld Moyglare Stud Farm
tb[1] 4 9-7
P J Smullen (130)

2 (9)
88-7526 **LORD ADMIRAL** (USA) [15] C
b h El Prado-Lady Ilsley
Charles O'Brien Mrs M V O'Brien
b 8 9-7
D P McDonogh (119)

3 (5)
11-1121 **FAME AND GLORY** [69] CD
b c Montjeu-Gryada
A P O'Brien Derrick Smith
3 9-0
J Murtagh (133)

4 (1)
1243-1 **GRAND DUCAL** (IRE) [104] D
b c Danehill Dancer-Mood Swings
A P O'Brien Mrs John Magnier
3 9-0
C O'Donoghue (109)

5 (8)
35-8113 **LOCH LONG** (IRE) [14] D
b c Galileo-Spinney
Tracey Collins Thistle Bloodstock Limited
3 9-0
P Shanahan (98)

6 (7)
14-5112 **MASTERCRAFTSMAN** (IRE) [18]
gr c Danehill Dancer-Starlight Dreams
A P O'Brien Derrick Smith
3 9-0
J A Heffernan (136)

7 (6)
1310948 **ROCKHAMPTON** (IRE) [42] CD
b c Galileo-Green Rosy
A P O'Brien Mrs John Magnier
3 9-0
S M Levey (106)

8 (2)
11-1111 **SEA THE STARS** (IRE) [18] CD
b c Cape Cross-Urban Sea
John M Oxx Christopher Tsui
3 9-0
M J Kinane (141)

9 (4)
-400023 **SET SAIL** (IRE) [18]
ch c Danehill Dancer-Ahdaab
A P O'Brien Derrick Smith
3 9-0
J P O'Brien (115)

2008 (8 ran) New Approach (5) J S Bolger 3 9-0 8/13F   K J Manning RPR122

BETTING FORECAST: 10-11 Sea The Stars, 13-8 Fame And Glory, 9-2 Mastercraftsman, 12 Casual Conquest, 40 Grand Ducal, 50 Lord Admiral, 150 Loch Long, 200 Rockhampton, 250 Set Sail.

Previous spread: *Hero's welcome.*

B y now the run-up to any race in which Sea The Stars was due to take part was becoming as predictable as the outcome, with 'will-he-won't-he?' stories eating up the column inches as the weather forecasters delivered their prognostications. And so it was in the days approaching the Leopardstown programme featuring the Tattersalls Millions Irish Champion Stakes, a race of huge value and prestige which in 2009 had extra significance: this was the first time during the season that Ireland's racehorse of the year – increasingly likely to be Ireland's racehorse of all time – would be running in his homeland.

Eventually given the go-ahead, Sea The Stars had eight horses taking him on, a mere five of whom were trained by Aidan O'Brien. Significantly, the Ballydoyle brigade was headed by not one but two serious contenders: Mastercraftsman again, and Fame And Glory, who since finishing second to Sea The Stars at Epsom had taken advantage of the Oxx colt's absence to land the Dubai Duty Free Irish Derby in fine style, finishing five lengths clear of stablemate Golden Sword, with the Oxx colt Mourayan third. The Ballydoyle camp was evidently so keen to lower Sea The Stars' colours that over ten furlongs at Leopardstown they would field both their main miler in Mastercraftsman and their main middle-distance performer in Fame And Glory. There was no doubt about it: Sea The Stars would have his work cut out.

Unusually for what is so often a major international contest, in 2009 all the runners in the Irish Champion Stakes were trained in Ireland. Grand Ducal, Rockhampton and Set Sail were doing their bit for the Aidan O'Brien cause. Another O'Brien – Charles, no relation to Aidan but son of the legendary Vincent O'Brien, who had died a few days before the Derby – trained Lord Admiral, who ran in the colours of his mother, Vincent's widow Jacqueline.

Then there was the four-year-old Casual Conquest, trained by Dermot Weld, a top-class colt who earlier in the year had won the Tattersalls Gold Cup at the Curragh and most recently

Last-minute consultation for John Oxx.

had landed the Royal Whip on the same course; Tracey Collins-trained Loch Long, who had won two minor races earlier in the season; and Sea The Stars, the scale of whose task was reflected in his starting price of 4-6 (as opposed to 1-4 at York). Fame And Glory started at 9-4, Mastercraftsman at 6-1; next in the betting was Casual Conquest on 16-1, with Grand Ducal on 100-1 and the other four on 150-1.

On the morning of the race, James Willoughby set the scene for yet another famous showdown between Ballydoyle and Sea The Stars . . .

Appearance of Stars will guarantee 'race of the season' billing

JAMES WILLOUGHBY
5 September 2009

THE news last night that John Oxx had walked the Leopardstown course and, with the proviso that the track is not subject to any unexpected rainfall overnight rainfall, declared Sea The Stars a probable runner in the Tattersalls Millions Irish Champion Stakes today, is what all racing fans had hoped for.

Oxx's final decision, whatever that may be, must be respected. He is a deeply thoughtful man and knows what is best for his horses, but Sea The Stars hacked up in his maiden on soft ground, his dam Urban Sea won the Arc on heavy ground, and his half-brother Galileo loved it also, so I personally have no worries on that score anyway.

Also, Leopardstown is a free-draining track and the executive have gone to the trouble to move the Champion to the outer track, further helping put life back into the surface. For a horse whose trademark has been adaptability, it would be odd to see him forced to duck the biggest challenge he has faced.

What a race this is set up to be. When people talk about maximising the sport's appeal to the public, their ideas are coarse compared with the finer delight that can be sampled by the purist here.

Given Sea The Stars runs, this is throroughbred racing on the Flat at the absolute peak of what it can deliver: brilliant racehorses with different characteristics stretched to their limit.

And humans will be tested too; tested for skill, for knowledge, for judgement on and off the track. What's more, there is a back story, for this very race has showcased the impact that tactics can have in the great clashes between champions, as with Fantastic Light and Galileo in 2001.

Godolphin outsmarted Aidan O'Brien on that occasion, but they also possibly gave him the stencil to turn the trick on Sea The Stars today. That's not to say that Fame And Glory or Mastercraftsman will definitely be nipping up the inside of their pacemakers on the home turn this afternoon, only that it exists as a precedent.

Sea The Stars will today have to fend off everything that O'Brien and Ballydoyle can throw at him. Fame And Glory and Mastercraftsman have won six Group 1s between them, and either could have been lauded as the best of their generation in any other year.

Their challenge is arguably greater than the sum of its parts. Aided by the presence of three stablemates, who are patently not good enough to challenge Sea The Stars, their different styles of running will provide a two-dimensional threat to the favourite.

As we saw at York, Mastercraftsman is a formidable galloper who can take even the best to the edge of the envelope. If he runs the same way as in the Juddmonte International Stakes, it is reasonable to expect that Sea The Stars will again have to work to pass him.

This time, however, there should be an additional threat. Fame And Glory has bottomless stamina and lots and lots of class. Those closest to him will swear he is a better horse now than when Sea The Stars sucker-punched him with a turn of speed in the slowly run Investec Derby at Epsom.

Moreover, Fame And Glory is a late-runner, a builder who comes calling late and has the power to overwhelm any horse if the pace up front is fast enough. If you talk to people who really know their stuff when it comes to sectional times, they will tell you that what this colt did in the Dubai Duty Free Irish Derby was sensational.

The pace was brutal at the Curragh and it told. Fame And Glory showed the side of his talent that we knew was always there but had not yet been fully exposed. Class in the racehorse may be exhibited by speed, acceleration or generosity, but it is the ability to withstand demanding fractions that is its nearest and neatest approximation.

Of course, the Irish Derby was over 1m4f. Montjeu, the sire of Fame And Glory, is the pre-eminent Derby sire of his time because he delivers incredible stamina to his offspring. This means his stock tend to be more effective over 1m4f than today's 1m2f, but that tendency can be offset if the pace is strong enough to test the field's sustained pace to the full.

How will O'Brien draw up his battle plan? How will his jockeys execute it? And, fundamentally, can a horse as brilliant as Sea The Stars be brought to earth by the combination of human thinking and equine athletic ability? This is a race that may define the career of the combatants more than anything that comes after.

It is a race of which Irish racing and Ireland should be proud, for it underlines the stature of the Irish Champion Stakes and the quality of the thoroughbreds trained in the country.

To reach the level it has, the Irish Champion has been greatly aided by the commitment of the top Irish Flat trainers to make it a target for their best horses.

With Sea The Stars in the field, this really will be the race of the season.

'I've ridden some great horses but this fellow's the best'

TONY O'HEHIR
6 September 2009

AFTER all the doubts about his participation, Sea The Stars produced arguably the best performance of his brilliant season by blowing away the opposition to stretch his Group 1-winning run to five in the Tattersalls Millions Irish Champion Stakes.

The Qatar Prix de l'Arc de Triomphe could be next for the season's star performer and Ladbrokes make him 6-4 favourite while Coral go 2-1 (from 4).

A delighted, and relieved, Oxx said: 'In the end the decision to run was an easy enough one to make. The ground wasn't ideal but it was good to yielding and we were happy to let him run.

'He has again shown that he is an exceptional colt and if the ground is suitable at Longchamp, then the Arc could be his next race. You wouldn't call running in a Group 1 every month since May, as this horse has done, a typical Arc preparation.

'But Sea The Stars has taken all his races really well this year and seems to be thriving. He is heavier now than he was earlier in the season and he showed today that he is really on top of his game.'

And how the Leopardstown crowd appreciated what they saw as Sea The Stars, who was 4-6 favourite, romped to victory.

Sea The Stars comes away from Fame And Glory and Mastercraftsman.

SLIM O'NEILL

assistant trainer

'For me, the Irish Champion was the day that he told everybody, "I am the best." I always felt proud to be associated with him, but that day was really special.'

The cheering continued as Oxx's star colt returned to the number one spot and was renewed when the world's best racehorse was led away.

A beaming Mick Kinane had waved to the crowd, standing ten deep around the unsaddling area, and then raised his left fist in salute, acknowledging the huge reception rarely given to a Flat race winner.

It was Kinane's seventh win in Ireland's highest-profile Flat race and it came 20 years after his first on Carroll House. Kinane said: 'Sea The Stars has got great receptions in England, but this one more than matched any of those. I've been lucky to ride some great horses, but this fellow is the best I've ridden.

'When the Ballydoyle pacemakers began to drop back and Mastercraftsman began to weaken, I was happy to sit and wait when Johnny [Murtagh] went around me before the straight. I didn't want to commit at that stage and when I decided to go my horse did the job really well.'

And, paying tribute to the Leopardstown management and staff, Kinane said: 'Full marks to everyone at Leopardstown for providing two tracks today and doing everything possible to provide the best conditions they could.'

Sea The Stars swept past Fame And Glory over one furlong out and was soon in full control of the race, winning as Oxx said 'quite easily for him' by two and a half lengths. It was the widest margin the son of Cape Cross has won by since he landed his maiden – the first of seven straight wins – by the same distance at Leopardstown in August of last year. The Emirates Airlines Champion Stakes is another race Oxx will consider for Sea The Stars, but the trainer was reluctant to look beyond the colt's next race, wherever that will be.

He said: 'Don't even ask me about the Breeders' Cup. Santa Anita is a long way away and it would be a hell of an ask for a horse who was trained for the 2,000 Guineas in May.

'It could be a bridge too far, but let's wait and see. There are other races to be considered before then. If it was to happen then I'd imagine it would probably be the Classic, but it is not a matter that concerns us now.'

Summing up the day and Sea The Stars' authoritative victory, Oxx said: 'We would have been very disappointed if he hadn't run today, just as we were very disappointed when he missed the Irish Derby because of the ground.

'It wasn't looking good a couple of days ago, but conditions improved considerably since Wednesday night and everything worked out well on the day. I leave the tactics to Mick and while we expected Fame And Glory to come at us late rather than early, he went first and Mick decided to wait.'

Sea The Stars' owner Christopher Tsui was an absentee due to business commitments in the US and the doubts until yesterday about the horse running.

But not all of the racing world that weekend was as joyous as Leopardstown, and Alastair Down's reflections on the race closed with mention of the deaths of two young apprentice jockeys in a fire at Malton, North Yorkshire …

163

The hero marches on – better, stronger and greater

ALASTAIR DOWN
6 September 2009

AS Sea The Stars finally stood in the place of honour on home soil in the Leopardstown winner's enclosure, a hand gripped my shoulder and an excited voice eulogised 'great horse, isn't he?' as the speaker shot through and ducked and dived his way through the throng to grasp John Oxx's hand.

Our man had business elsewhere tending to the second and third, but Aidan O'Brien, who has been whacked over the head that often by Sea The Stars this year that he must indeed be seeing stars by now, was not going to let a small matter such as defeat stand in the way of the expression of his admiration.

He had just fired off a five-strong flight of tactical missiles in the hope of finding some way to bring Sea The Stars to earth, but to no avail.

Despite the best efforts of Ballydoyle's massed bands of pacesetters and heavyweight assassins of the calibre of Mastercraftsman and Fame And Glory, frankly Sea The Stars never even looked vulnerable here as he extended his Group 1 run to five in front of a happily starstruck and appreciative Leopardstown crowd for some of whom the journey would have been worth the trek barefoot.

I am not sure I have ever stood in the paddock before a major race and wished so fervently with every fibre that a

particular horse did not get beat. And I would wager that feeling was echoed by most of the huge crowd that packed the back-of-stand balconies and stood stacks deep around the parade ring and lining the horse's route out on to the course. The pre-race air had that edge of great deeds afoot that only the very rare clash of indisputably good horses can summon up. We were on the edge of seeing one of the all-time benchmarks put to the test once more and asked yet again to put his pre-eminence beyond doubt.

I have been lucky enough to see every one of this colt's runs at three as he has flicked his way effortlessly up through the categories of esteem from Guineas-winning colt of rich promise to the level of the immutably magnificent. 'A landmark horse,' said John Oxx, 'the sort who comes along every 20 years or so and you always remember them.'

Well Oxx may be underselling Sea The Stars, as I'm not sure there has been one of mighty stamp every couple of decades over the last two or three centuries. In fact this extraordinary colt, who carries a prizefighter's punch but has the temperament of a professor, looks greater by the outing.

Sea The Stars looked so rudely well beforehand it bordered on the actionable, and I restate my long-held view that even someone who can't tell the difference between a horse and the town hall clock need take only one look at this one to know he is something different.

Nothing gets to him during the preliminaries. When the wordsmiths coined 'unflappable' and 'unfazed' they might have had this horse in mind. But forget the preliminaries – the important point is that nothing gets to him in the race.

I have the slight impression that Oxx, for all the breathless pressure of handling this phenomenon, is looking a couple of years younger than at the start of the season. But if that is debatable, I insist the years are falling off Mick Kinane and that he is plummeting joyously back through his 40s, 30s and 20s to become a teenager again. Poor feller will be

GRACE CANNIFFE
equine massage therapist
'The Irish Champion Stakes is my best memory of Sea The Stars in action, because I was there. All year I'd been watching his races on television, and at Leopardstown I could hardly believe that I was actually part of the occasion. I took my mother with me, and we just couldn't believe how emotional the whole thing was. He was such a part of my life, and that day was just amazing.'

having to deal with the onset of puberty if they keep running this horse.

And it is clear that running and giving him plenty to do is an absolute essential if you are to keep any sort of grip on the supernova of his talent. This colt does not eat, as Oxx says, 'he devours his food' and 'he needs to work.'

Yesterday, Sea The Stars was heavier than ever this season and, in his case, this is a good thing. He is like a furnace: the more you stoke him up and fuel him, the greater the power he produces.

I lost count of the times folk came up to me on-course late in the day and asked if I had ever seen a better horse, and the fact the question was on so many lips tells the telling tale. Here, as far as the public are concerned, is a piece of contemporary magic, in our here and now, against whom nearly all others of times past can be measured and found to come up short.

Among the many Irish race fans who had made the journey to watch Sea The Stars yesterday was an interloper from Britain, a fine judge of a horse but a jumps man to his boot-straps who is not sure Flat racing is not some strange activity that should be left to consenting adults in private. But he had come over to Ireland because he wasn't going to let this treasure slip through the fingers of his experience of the exceptional.

And he too was duly smitten by this horse, though, in fairness, his excitement did drop a peg or two when it was patiently explained to him that Sea The Stars may next run in the Arc and not the Arkle.

This was an afternoon when a reputation was cemented anew at the most elevated level. It was magnificent and nourishing. But it was just a horserace.

Away to the east, across the water in a core North Yorkshire racing town, two lives every ounce of which were bent on seeing such days as these for untold years to come were brought to a fearful and sickening end.

There are no words for such a tragedy. Just a resigned and sorry sadness.

167

....

ANALYSIS

Graham Dench

SEA THE STARS' only appearance on home soil all year appropriately came in Ireland's most significant race, but the eagerly anticipated rematch with Derby runner-up Fame And Glory and Juddmonte runner-up Mastercraftsman almost did not happen owing to fears that that the ground might be too soft for him. Fortunately John Oxx's decision to commit Sea The Stars after an improvement in the weather and an extraordinary effort on the part of the Leopardstown groundstaff was gloriously vindicated, for the event delivered a superb spectacle and the highpoint in ratings terms of this magnificent thoroughbred's career.

This was without doubt Sea The Stars' toughest assignment to date. Either Fame And Glory and Mastercraftsman would have been a worthy champion three-year-old most years and, with three possible pacemakers in the field to support the two Ballydoyle principals, it had the makings of a tactical nightmare for Mick Kinane.

Set Sail and Rockhampton went about their work with zeal, and although Fame And Glory was initially held up behind Sea The Stars he began to bring his stamina into play when moving up three out and then going to the front as the pacemakers dropped away, and as his stablemate Mastercraftsman, who led only briefly, also began to feel the strain. Kinane, however, readily covered the move, and the race was soon won. Sea The Stars led with more than a furlong to go and came away to score comfortably by two and a half lengths, with little sign of the idling in front that had marked some of his earlier performances.

It was a most emphatic performance, and one which both Oxx and Kinane had little hesitation in agreeing was his best so far. It's no wonder either, for Sea The Stars' Racing Post Rating of 138 here equalled that recorded by Daylami when a runaway nine-length winner of the corresponding race ten years previously, and that mark was the best recorded on turf in the 22 years for which the paper's database holds details. It bettered by fully 7lb the mark awarded to Fantastic Light after his epic defeat of Sea The Stars' half-brother Galileo in the 2001 Irish Champion, and by 10lb Dylan Thomas' first and better win in the same race in 2006.

It was also a display that increased the likelihood of Sea The Stars running in the Prix de l'Arc de Triomphe, for while the ground had dried out significantly since mid-week, it was still on the soft side and yet he clearly handled it well.

The margin back to Fame And Glory, who had been so ruthlessly effective in the Irish Derby, was a bit wider than it had been at Epsom, and this time there was little room for argument: Fame And Glory was very much second best, albeit having once again run most honourably in defeat.

Some felt that Mastercraftsman had not quite got home when beaten by Sea The Stars at York, and that view gained further credibility here, for having got to the front briefly before Fame And Glory he was unable to sustain his effort at the end of a race run at a searching pace. He went on to win over a little further on Polytrack at Dundalk, but that was in a relatively modest Group 3 in which he was simply different class.

The rest were left trailing upwards of nine lengths behind Mastercraftsman.

LEOPARDSTOWN (L-H)
Saturday, September 5
OFFICIAL GOING: Good to yielding
The 2.40, 3.50, 4.30 and 5.35 were run on the outer track, the rest on the inner.

5688a	**TATTERSALLS MILLIONS IRISH CHAMPION STKS (GROUP 1)**	**1m 2f**
	3:50 (3:50) 3-Y-O+	

£552,427 (£183,495; £86,407; £28,155; £18,446; £8,737)

RPR

1		**Sea The Stars (IRE)**[18] 5135 3-9-0 133................................ MJKinane 2	138+

(John M Oxx, Ire) *settled bhd ldrs: 5th 1/2-way: hdwy in 3rd 2f out: pushed out to ld over 1f out: kpt on strly fnl f: comf*   **4/6**[1]

2	2 ½	**Fame And Glory**[69] 3438 3-9-0 126...................................... JMurtagh 5	131

(A P O'Brien, Ire) *hld up: 7th 1/2-way: hdwy in 3rd 3f out: rdn to chal 2f out: sn led: hdd over 1f out: no ex and kpt on same pce fnl f*   **9/4**[2]

3	2 ½	**Mastercraftsman (IRE)**[18] 5135 3-9-0 127...................... JAHeffernan 7	126

(A P O'Brien, Ire) *chsd ldrs: 3rd 1/2-way: hdwy in 2nd 3f out: rdn to ld briefly over 2f out: hdd under 2f out: no ex in 3rd over 1f out: kpt on same pce*   **6/1**[3]

4	9	**Grand Ducal (IRE)**[104] 2306 3-9-0 107.......................... CO'Donoghue 1	108

(A P O'Brien, Ire) *chsd ldrs: 4th 1/2-way: rdn in 5th 3f out: no imp in 4th under 2f out: kpt on same pce*   **100/1**

5	4 ½	**Lord Admiral (USA)**[15] 5231 8-9-7 108.....................(b) DPMcDonogh 9	99

(Charles O'Brien, Ire) *hld up towards rr: hdwy to 6th 3f out: rdn and no ex 2f out: kpt on same pce*   **150/1**

6	5	**Loch Long (IRE)**[14] 5277 3-9-0 96.. PShanahan 8	89

(Tracey Collins, Ire) *disp early: sn chsd ldrs: pushed along in 6th 1/2-way: rr 3f out: kpt on one pce*   **150/1**

7	½	**Casual Conquest (IRE)**[20] 5076 4-9-7 121.................(bt1) PJSmullen 3	88

(D K Weld, Ire) *dwlt: hld up towards rr: rdn in 7th 3f out: no imp 2f out: kpt on one pce*   **16/1**

8	19	**Rockhampton (IRE)**[42] 4298 3-9-0 100................................ SMLevey 6	50

(A P O'Brien, Ire) *sn rdn to chse ldrs: disp after 3f: 2nd 1/2-way: rdn and wknd over 3f out*   **150/1**

9	4	**Set Sail (IRE)**[18] 5135 3-9-0 102.. JPO'Brien 4	42

(A P O'Brien, Ire) *sn led: disp after 3f out: rdn and hdd over 2f out: no ex and wknd*   **150/1**

2m 3.90s (-4.30) **Going Correction** +0.20s/f (Good)
WFA 3 from 4yo+ 7lb   **9** Ran   SP% **114.6**
Speed ratings: **125,123,121,113,110 106,105,90,87**
 CSF £2.38 TOTE £2.00: £1.10, £1.30, £1.30; DF 2.60.
Owner Christopher Tsui **Bred** Sunderland Holdings **Trained** Currabeg, Co Kildare

PRIX DE L'ARC DE TRIOMPHE

4 October 2009

3.15 Qatar Prix de l'Arc de Triomphe (Group 1) (3yo+ Colts & Fillies) BBC2
Winner £2,219,029   1m4f

For 3yo+ Entries 20 Penalty value 1st £2,219,029 2nd £887,767 3rd £443,883 4th £221,748 5th £111,068

No	Form	Horse		Weight	Jockey	RPR
1 (1)	32-4233	**YOUMZAIN** (IRE) [28]	b h Sinndar-Sadima	v[1] 6 9-5	K Fallon	(137)
		M R Channon (GB)	Jaber Abdullah			
2 (12)	111-231	**CONDUIT** (IRE) [71]	ch c Dalakhani-Well Head	4 9-5	Ryan Moore	(137)
		Sir Michael Stoute (GB)	Ballymacoll Stud			
3 (9)	15-3112	**VISION D'ETAT** (FR) [21]	b c Chichicastenango-Uberaba	4 9-5	O Peslier	(133)
		E Libaud	Jacques Detre			
4 (17)	03-1135	**MAGADAN** (IRE) [98]	b c High Chaparral-Molasses	4 9-5	A Crastus	(126)
		E Lellouche	Ecurie Wildenstein			
5 (18)	34-2555	**THE BOGBERRY** (USA) [28]	ch c Hawk Wing-Lahinch	4 9-5	M Kappushev	(125)
		A de Royer-Dupre	S Efros			
6 (7)	-243785	**STEELE TANGO** (USA) [92]	ch c Okawango-Waltzing Around	4 9-5	Darryll Holland	(122)
		R A Teal (GB)	The Thirty Acre Racing Partnership			
7 (3)	88-2121	**GETAWAY** (GER) [28]	b h Monsun-Guernica	6 9-5	S Pasquier	(134)
		J Hirschberger (GER)	Baron G Von Ullmann			
8 (13)	4-77522	**TULLAMORE** (USA) [63]	b c Theatrical-Bungalow	4 9-5	V Janacek	(111)
		Z Koplik (CZE)	Yoko Cz Sro			
9 (4)	22-1125	**HOT SIX** (BRZ) [63]	gr c Burooj-Babysix	4 9-4	T J Pereira	
		G Duarte (BRZ)	Estrela Energia Stables			
10 (2)	23-2111d	**DAR RE MI** (GB)	b f Singspiel-Darara	4 9-2	Jimmy Fortune	(131)
		J H M Gosden (GB)	Lord Lloyd-Webber			
11 (11)	4-34949	**TANGASPEED** (FR) [21]	b f Vertical Speed-Fitanga	4 9-2	I Mendizabal	(121)
		R Laplanche	R Pires & Mme L Gagneux			
12 (8)	-924353	**LA BOUM** (GER) [42]	br m Monsun-La Bouche	6 9-2	T Jarnet	(118)
		Robert Collet	E Trussardi			
13 (15)	-11462	**BEHESHTAM** (FR) [21]	ch c Peintre Celebre-Behkara	3 8-11	G Mosse	(125)
		A de Royer-Dupre	H H Aga Khan			
14 (14)	4000239	**SET SAIL** (IRE) [29]	ch c Danehill Dancer-Ahdaab	3 8-11	S M Levey	(118)
		A P O'Brien (IRE)	D Smith, Mrs J Magnier, M Tabor			
15 (10)	1-11212	**FAME AND GLORY** (IRE) [29]	b c Montjeu-Gryada	3 8-11	J Murtagh	(141)
		A P O'Brien (IRE)	D Smith, Mrs J Magnier, M Tabor			
16 (19)	1-42111	**CAVALRYMAN** (FR) [21]	b c Halling-Silversword	3 8-11	L Dettori	(131)
		A Fabre	Godolphin S N C			
17 (5)	1243-14	**GRAND DUCAL** (IRE) [29]	b c Danehill Dancer-Mood Swings	3 8-11	P J Smullen	(118)
		A P O'Brien (IRE)	Mrs John Magnier, M Tabor & D Smith			
18 (6)	1-11111	**SEA THE STARS** (IRE) [29]	b c Cape Cross-Urban Sea	3 8-11	M J Kinane	(147)
		John M Oxx (IRE)	Christopher Tsui			
19 (16)	1-11111	**STACELITA** (FR) [21]	b f Monsun-Soignee	3 8-8	J-C Rouget	(135)
			M Schwartz & Ecurie Monastic			

2008 (16 ran) Zarkava (Ire) (1) A de Royer-Dupre 3 8-8 13/8F   C Soumillon PM129

BETTING FORECAST: 8-11 Sea The Stars, 6 Fame And Glory, 8 Conduit, 12 Cavalryman, 14 Vision D'Etat, 16 Stacelita, 20 Youmzain, 22 Dar Re Mi, 33 Beheshtam, Getaway, 150 Magadan, 200 Hot Six, 250 Grand Ducal, 300 La Boum, The Bogberry, 500 bar.

Previous spread: *250 metres to go.*

And so to Paris, for Europe's most prestigious horserace, the Qatar Prix de l'Arc de Triomphe. Throughout the season there had been alternative races in mind should the primary target be ruled out by the rain gods, but after Leopardstown there were, in reality, only two left: the Arc in Paris on 4 October and the Breeders' Cup Classic at Santa Anita, California, five weeks later. It was possible that Sea The Stars could contest both, and it was undeniable that winning the USA's biggest all-aged race would hugely endear him to American breeders; on the other hand, running in California would involve a lengthy journey, the horse had been on the go since the spring with little respite, he would be racing on an unfamiliar surface rather than grass, etc. The Prix de l'Arc de Triomphe would be the main target, and the issue of the Breeders' Cup could be addressed after that.

The customary fears about the weather and therefore the Longchamp ground again dominated the days leading up to the race, but halfway through pre-Arc week it started to look odds-on that Sea The Stars would take his chance, and suddenly there was no space at all on bespoke travel packages for that weekend in Paris. Even work rider Alex da Silva, determined to be on the spot when his 'best friend' had his ultimate date with destiny, had to settle for a pre-dawn flight from Dublin to Paris on the big day.

It was a characteristically strength-in-depth Arc field. Of the nineteen runners, seven were three-year-olds, with Sea The Stars being opposed by old rival Fame And Glory, who had two pacemakers in the shape of Grand Ducal and Set Sail; by Cavalryman, trained by seven-times Arc winning trainer Andre Fabre and ridden by Frankie Dettori, a colt who had won his last three races, notably the Grand Prix de Paris and the Prix Niel, invariably a significant Arc trial; by the Aga Khan's colt Behestam, runner-up to Cavalryman in the Prix Niel; and by the filly Stacelita, whose brilliant wins in the Prix Saint-Alary and Prix de Diane had invoked comparisons with the great *filly Zarkava, sensational winner of the 2008 Arc, but who last time had won the Prix Vermeille only on the controversial disqualification of Dar Re Mi for interference.*

Four-year-old Dar Re Mi, owned by Andrew Lloyd Webber and trained by John Gosden, was looking to put the record straight with Stacelita in the Arc, but the strongest fancied of the older horses was Conduit, third to Sea The Stars in the Eclipse and then a doughty winner of the King George at Ascot. Another four-year-old with a realistic chance was Vision d'Etat, trained by Eric Libaut. Vision d'Etat had won the Prix du Jockey-Club in 2008 and the Prince of Wales's Stakes at Royal Ascot earlier in 2009 and finished runner-up in the Prix Foy three weeks before the Arc, and was presumably not aware of the fact that no French-trained older horse had won the Longchamp showpiece since Sea The Stars' dam Urban Sea back in 1993.

Six-year-old Youmzain, trained by Mick Channon, was an old Arc hand who had finished second in both the last two runnings – to Dylan Thomas in 2007 and Zarkava in 2008 – but despite being narrowly beaten by Ask in the Coronation Cup had failed to win a race in 2009, and another six-year-old with a similar chance was German-trained Getaway, winner at Group 1 level at Dusseldorf in July and Baden-Baden in September but already twice beaten in the Arc. Of the rest, particular interest attached to the four-year-old Hot Six, who had come all the way from Brazil, where he had won the Gran Premio Latinamericano in March.

Rarely in recent memory had a race on the Flat generated such keen anticipation. This was to be one of those days when almost everyone wanted a particular horse to win, a mood caught by both Steve Dennis in the Racing Post *on the morning of the race.*

Only one Arc result that would really fit the bill

STEVE DENNIS

4 October 2009

AT JUST before 3.15 this afternoon he'll be squeezed into stall six, the gates will be pressed shut behind him, and he'll be left to get on with it himself. What Sea The Stars does in the following two and a half minutes will define him as a racehorse.

People aren't ardently discussing him in the aisles of the local supermarket, because he hasn't made the leap from racing icon to household name and never will, no matter how hard we wish it were different, but everyone with a media mouthpiece or a forum log-in has had their two-penn'orth about Sea The Stars.

Whether he is the best in 20 years, 30 years, 40 years or since the Darley Arabian covered his first mare is a subject that has occupied most people's minds at some stage of the season. It's not important at all, on most levels. Is he better than Nijinsky, or Dancing Brave, or Mill Reef, or Sea-Bird? Who cares? He's just another brown horse and in six months' time we'll have another brown horse to get all frothy about and Sea The Stars will begin the long and irreversible process of receding into history.

On another level, of course, it's very important indeed. Horseracing is built on a ranking system – this horse is better than that one, no he isn't, okay let's have a race and see – and one of the delights of the sport is to ransack the memories for great horses in order to find the right place for the latest member of the club.

In the paddock, with Jack O'Shea joining John Lynes at the head of affairs.

Sea The Stars will be ranked accordingly when he retires, win or lose today, but victory at Longchamp carries more weight than others. Winning the Juddmonte International is all very well, as is the Irish Champion Stakes, but Arc success confers a cachet of prowess that few races own. It's the great end-of-year championship, a climactic crucible in which reputations are either case-hardened against mortality or irreparably broken.

Many are broken. Nijinsky was beaten, Troy was beaten, Reference Point was beaten, Generous was beaten, Deep Impact was beaten. Some come through the fire unaltered – Sea-Bird, Mill Reef, Dancing Brave. The latter's Arc victory is still fresh in my memory. Watching on television at home, I became so concerned about his non-appearance on camera that I left my chair and edged towards the screen on my knees, an unconscious supplication for information. By the time he arrived in vision I was up close to the screen, not silent with awe but shouting with delight.

That's what we look for, we whose hours are counted out under the spell of racehorses. We want to howl with joy, we want to push the man standing next to us and shout, 'Did you see that?' in his ear. We want great champions.

Great champions necessarily have a rarity value. In the USA, they have been waiting for a Triple Crown winner for 31 years, and every time they seem to be closing in on the holy grail something crops up to prevent it. This year we thought we might have a Triple Crown winner – does anyone seriously think that Sea The Stars wouldn't have beaten Mastery? – but other decisions were made, other paths trodden, and they have led us to where we wait today, under the plane trees on the Bois de Boulogne.

In the build-up to the Arc, I have achieved a very slight connection with several of the contenders. I interviewed Christophe Lemaire, so a little part of me will be pleased if Stacelita wins, even though injury has robbed poor Lemaire of his big day. I wrote about Youmzain, so there's another small part of me that would be happy to see him win.

Earlier this year I went to Ballymacoll Stud, so a Conduit victory would be a cause of some small satisfaction.

Any of the three would be a worthy winner, as would Fame And Glory, Cavalryman, Vision d'Etat or Dar Re Mi if destiny decreed it. But there is only one result that would really fit the bill, that would have us creeping towards our television on our knees.

If Sea The Stars wins the Arc it will confirm his perfect season, a season that blossomed in spring, reached full bloom in the summer and ripened gloriously in the autumn. Now and again we need the right result, the outcome fervently hoped for, the chance to wipe away years of disappointments with one sun-yellow flash of silk, one bright bay arrow speeding for the bullseye.

There's plenty of room for things to go wrong in life, plenty of time for failure. Opportunities to get it right, truly right, are so few and so far between that when it does happen it enriches us all, provides a holy jolt of what's good for us.

Today there's a chance for that to happen.

Do it right, Sea The Stars. Win this race.

'No horse has the speed he has'

JON LEES
5 October 2009

SEA THE STARS spent the year matching the feats of horseracing's most illustrious names. Yesterday he raised the bar to a new level to cement a unique place in racing history.

Arguments will rage over the merits of racing's greatest champions, but none can boast the record of the extraordinary Sea The Stars, who rose magnificently to the challenge of becoming the only horse to win the 2,000 Guineas, Derby and Qatar Prix de l'Arc de Triomphe before a rapturous crowd at Longchamp. The Arc giants, including Sea-Bird, Mill Reef and Dancing Brave, enjoyed the benefit of a mid-campaign break. It proved a race too far for Nijinsky. Yet Sea The Stars maintained a metronomic momentum to clinch his sixth Group 1 victory in a row, achieved at a rate of one per month.

The opportunity to add a seventh, the Breeders' Cup Classic, was left open by owner Christopher Tsui and trainer John Oxx but, on his performances in Europe, Sea The Stars may have already proved himself without peer.

In triumph he emulated his dam Urban Sea, who won the Arc in 1993 for Tsui's parents David and Ling, while jockey Mick Kinane has clinched his three victories in 1989 (Carroll House), 1999 (Montjeu) and 2009.

Winning the world's richest turf race is a pinnacle in itself, but the additional weight of history proved no extra burden on the shoulders of the colt or his veteran rider. The jockey's brow may have been furrowed as the pair drew bursts of cheers and applause as they circled the parade ring before the race, but on the track Kinane betrayed no hint of concern.

Even when Kinane had to sacrifice a prominent early position

ALEX DA SILVA

exercise rider

'The Arc was my best memory. I had to go and see my friend, so I bought a ticket the day before the race and got the flight at 5 o'clock in the morning. I said to him before the race: You go and win today. And after he had won I went and saw him, my very good friend, and my heart talked to him for a long, long time.'

to settle the headstrong Sea The Stars behind other horses and risk the possibility of running into traffic when it was time to go forward, there was no panic.

It was to leave Sea The Stars with significant ground to make up when the race unfolded in the straight, but once Kinane had identified a gap on the inside, Sea The Stars shot through it to strike the front a furlong out and cross the line two lengths clear of Youmzain (runner-up for a unique third time), who was a head in front of Cavalryman, with Conduit fourth.

'I thought after Leopardstown nothing could beat him,' said Oxx. 'He was the best horse by far, he'll win the Arc. But as you get closer and you think about the great horses who have come here after a busy season and not done it, you begin to think that he'd be just another one.

'He was in great form. We were delighted with his preparation. He seemed better than ever in his homework. His physical condition was getting better. Every week we'd see him at evening stables and he'd look stronger and more masculine, so we were hopeful he might improve.

'There was a bit of jostling early on and it set him off. He wanted to run a bit keen there for a while, a bit like the Derby. Mick had to pull him back, then to get him in behind horses and settle him. That left him in a position that I'm sure made the punters who backed him a bit nervous. He had some of the fancied horses just in front of him and there was a little bit of an anxious moment there, whether he was going to try to draw out or go in, but once he started to go you could see that he would get through.

'No horse in any race has the speed that he has. He's come on an awful lot since the Eclipse. He's a better horse now and again he does just enough when he hits the front. He'll never win by very far, but he's a great, great horse to keep winning all those races. It's just remarkable. I can't really believe it.'

Sea The Stars was cut to 4-6 (from 2-1) by William Hill and 4-5 (from 9-4) by Coral for the Breeders' Cup Classic but, with a

GARY WITHEFORD

horseman

'I've been lucky enough to have seen all Sea The Stars' races since the Guineas, but Arc day stands out. When he came through and the crowd lifted the roof off, it was unbelievable. I was just like a little ant in the masses, but it had been something for me to have been part of him starting out as a racehorse and to be part of that day was something else. Just brilliant!'

career at stud beckoning, a crack at the prize will be the subject of considerable discussion over what Tsui described as 'a very important decision'.

Oxx, who saddled the last Derby winner to win the Arc (Sinndar in 2000), was non-committal. 'We just go from race to race and see,' he said. 'He's done a lot. You're going to ask about the Breeders' Cup. It's 7 November. Now is not the time to make any decision about that. I can't see him staying in training next year but we haven't discussed anything.'

Kinane said: 'His coat has gone. He's got hairy today and you can see he got warm. I don't know what John and the owners have in mind. Does he need to achieve anything more? I don't know. It's questionable. He's a phenomenal horse. You'd hate to do anything wrong by him.'

Sea The Stars surges away from Stacelita (orange colours) and Cavalryman (no. 10).

Victory to set soul soaring as Arc hero joins the immortals

ALASTAIR DOWN

5 October 2009

ON A bow-wave of exultant acclamation, Sea The Stars swept all before him in the Arc yesterday with a stunning display of his superiority, not just over those opposing him at Longchamp of an October Sunday, but of virtually every thoroughbred in the 300 years that the species has trod the Earth.

And it was not just the fact of the victory but the manner of it that didn't merely lift the soul but set it soaring. For the sixth consecutive month, with the sort of reliability that makes the Greenwich Time Signal look over its shoulder, here was Sea The Stars doing what he does best – winning a Group 1.

It began when the buds of spring had yet to burst, over a mile at Newmarket off a squeezed preparation. Through high summer, over assorted trips and including the definitive physical test of Epsom, he kept delivering. And now, amid the browns and golds of autumn in the forcing of the Bois de Boulogne, he came up with perhaps the most compelling victory of all. Because if ever a race threatened to spiral off script and into tears, it was this one.

Having bounded out in second place, a combination of Mick Kinane wanting to restrain him and the horse getting jostled resulted in his getting lit up. He may exude all the competitiveness of your dozing grandma before the race, but he is some competitor once the stalls are opened – mad for the road and just itching to swing a punch – and it took time for Kinane to get the message through.

JOHN OXX

'Sea The Stars weighed around 524 kilos for the Derby and Eclipse and around 528 for the Irish Champion Stakes, and when we weighed him the evening before he left for Longchamp he was something like 538. I wasn't sure that the scales were giving us a proper reading. But we weren't worried that we'd let him get too heavy, as we knew he was fit.'

181

Above and right: *Coming back in triumph.*

Truth be told, by the time he was racing sweetly and on an even keel, Sea The Stars was in a bad place in a race in which in which location, location and location are usually all-important. Even Kinane admitted: 'I ended up in a position I maybe didn't want to be in.'

It was by no means a case of all hope being lost, but the last bloke in France to find himself in such an unpromising position was the Count of Monte Cristo. Kinane added: 'But this is a rare horse. He's exceptional – a phenomenon.'

Despite Sir Mark Prescott's maxim 'Whenever a jockey opens his mouth it is time to let your mind wander elsewhere', I urge you to give full weight to Kinane's words, and the choice of them. 'Rare, exceptional, a phenomenon' – can you argue with any of them? And consider the man who uttered them. These are not the silly spoutings of some young jockey

who needs to meet his razor only twice a week. Kinane sets the benchmark for grizzled and, at seen-it-all 50, is more seasoned than a seaside fence.

But the truly startling tribute Kinane paid to Sea The Stars had nothing to with words. What really knocked your socks off was the ride he gave him, because, as those of us in the stands began mentally to fret and fidget as the race unfolded, not a Kinane eyelid was batted, not even an eyebrow hair turned.

He was a picture of unconcern, not because he is a smart-ass or a show-off, but because in a lifetime of riding racehorses none has ever inspired a totality of confidence such as this one.

It was not that Sea The Stars was ever in a hopeless scrape but, as I watched, my exact thought was 'it only needs one

BROUGH SCOTT

'As with all truly great performances, the more you look at it the better it gets. For this was no early escape or deliberate waiting for the final trump. This was a swift and brutal and complete assertion of one horse's dominance over all the others. Because the final verdict was an eased-up two lengths over the weight-conceding Youmzain, (which on paper actually makes that older colt the superior), it is easy to miss quite how extraordinary had been the move. But look at Sea The Stars' positions at the 300 and 100 metre poles (helpfully marked in white on the BBC replay) and you can see him take five lengths out of the leader. That's a kick like Dancing Brave's – only harder.

'For you can't argue with the clock. In 1971 Mill Reef set a new track record at 2mins 28.3sec. In 1986 Dancing Brave lowered it to 2mins 27.7sec. This year, in what was not a fast run Arc, Sea The Stars came home in 2mins 26.3sec. In the Eclipse he set the fastest time in the 40 years of reliable clocking, and in the Juddmonte he set a new track record. Say what you like about the champions of today compared with those of the past, but don't anyone pretend that they are getting slower.'

thing to go wrong now and they're cooked.' But in fact it turned out that half a dozen things could have gone awry and he would still have won.

When Kinane finally demanded of the favourite that he go about the business of winning his race, the response was instant and awesome in the incredible smoothness with which a doubtful victory was turned into a certain one. Once he began his move, he looked insuperable – which is what he has been all season.

Sea The Stars hit the front over a furlong out, and how many Arcs have you seen in which pretty well nothing happened in the last 200 yards of what is usually a race fought out with feral ferocity? Sea The Stars simply put the Arc to bed with a furlong to run and nothing got near him.

Curiously, for a man quite closely involved with Sea The Stars, John Oxx seemed to have watched another race. 'I was quite happy throughout,' he said, 'he was always going well and with good horses round him. Three hundred metres out, it was all over.'

Not for the first time, it was hard not to give silent thanks that this horse has been matched with this man as his trainer. That is not a comment about other men, just that Oxx has

been more than equal to all the moments this horse has brought us.

It took plenty of time for the winner to return to unsaddle, but if Mick had elected to take him for a spin round the Place de la Concorde it wouldn't have mattered, as it would just have given the expectant paddock crowd time to brew up their welcome back.

And here, distilled into one horse, in one race, on an imperishable afternoon, the whole magnificent madness of racing not only made sense but, so much rarer, felt completely worthwhile. I'm not putting racing up against global warming or feeding the poor, but just sometimes it really does take flight to something much more than which horse runs fastest around a field.

In 1993, Urban Sea's victory was dismissed as 'l'Arc de Mickey Mouse', yet 16 years on her son has revised the old lists of the matchless, writing his name among the tiny handful of the undying.

They will wrangle over ratings, they will compare and contrast and hold the diamond of this horse up to the light in the search for flaws. That's fine. Let the mathematicians give us the wisdom, for it has its place. But, for me, what

What the experts said

WALTER SWINBURN
'You would have to say he's as good as there has been, but you can understand why I find it hard to separate him and Shergar. This horse has an exceptionally high cruising speed and looks as if he can cut them down whenever he wants. In all his races from half a mile out he's playing with them; you can see the confidence flowing through Mick's veins.'

THE AGA KHAN
'He's an exceptional horse.'

PAT EDDERY
'He was brilliant. He has run every month for the last six months and won six Group 1s in a row. They can go to America if they like but I just hope he never runs again. He has nothing left to prove.'

CRIQUETTE HEAD-MAAREK
'He's a fantastic horse. What he did today and what he has done all year is amazing. It's difficult to describe what you feel when you see a horse like Sea The Stars, but I know I have never seen a horse do what he did today. It's a dream to have a horse like him. Kinane and the horse make a perfect couple.'

will always matter is being at Longchamp in a crowd that beforehand was willing Sea The Stars not to be beaten, watched him flirt with the unthinkable as the drama began to boil, but emerge rampant at the business end of Europe's greatest race to grab his place with the immortals.

It is so rare to be able to look at a horse and know, in the very fibre of your soul, that generations of people come and go without the joy of seeing one remotely as good.

Few are so fortunate.

Sixteen years after Urban Sea, Christopher Tsui returns to the Arc winner's circle.

ANALYSIS
Graham Dench

By no means SEA THE STARS' best performance strictly from a ratings perspective, but in many respects the one that defines his qualities most completely, for little went right for him and he could so easily have been beaten. This time it was the style of his success rather than the substance, for it was a visually sensational effort.

Having carried all before him in England and Ireland, winning five times at the top level in five months, expectation was sky-high. However, despite being sent off a short-priced favourite, his task was a formidable one, on several counts. He was at a disadvantage in not having enjoyed a mid-season break, which has become the norm for Arc winners in recent years, and there were still some who doubted his stamina for a strongly run 1m4f. What's more, since Sea-Bird in 1965, only three horses had completed the Epsom Derby/Arc double in the same season (Mill Reef, Lammtarra and Sinndar), while 17 others had tried and failed, and only the great Dancing Brave in the previous 40 years had taken the Guineas en route.

A big field also threatened to make things tricky, but the ground had come right for him and he was also lucky with the draw. Once again, he went to post in top form after a trouble-free preparation, his most recent work having reportedly been his best ever.

With the Ballydoyle pacemakers Set Sail and Grand Ducal effectively ignored and the main pack following the no-more-than-fair pace set by the top French filly Stacelita, very little went right for Sea The Stars. Warm beforehand, he pulled for his head through the early stages and having got shuffled back in the pack as Kinane tried to restrain him he continued to race very keenly to the entrance to the straight. Hampered momentarily on straightening up before going for his run up the inside rail, he then found the tiring Grand Ducal falling back towards him. However, when Kinane deftly switched Sea The Stars he found the most electrifying turn of foot, one which took him from looking in real trouble to having the race won in just a matter of strides. He left Dar Re Mi and Stacelita for dead, and he was home and dried before Youmzain burst through the pack to snatch a third successive second place, ahead of the Grand Prix De Paris and Niel winner Cavalryman and the King George winner Conduit. He won with remarkable comfort in the circumstances, making top-class opponents look ordinary.

The first horse ever to complete the Guineas/Derby/Arc treble, Sea The Stars confirmed here that he had it all. It was a truly stunning performance, and one that will live long in the memory. Disappointment was understandable when a trip to Santa Anita for the Breeders' Cup Classic was ruled out and his retirement confirmed, but there could have been no better way for him to have brought down the curtain on a truly fabulous career.

Youmzain, visored for the first time, might not have enjoyed the success at the top level that his talents deserve, but he ran another screamer under his ideal conditions – a strongly-run 1m4f on fast ground. He was beaten the same distance here as he had been beaten by Zarkava 12 months earlier.

Cavalryman was following the route taken by the 2006 Arc winner Rail Link, who was also from the Fabre stable. The Niel has been much the best trial for the Arc in recent years and Cavalryman boasted the classic French preparation. Considering he was badly drawn in stall 19, he did well to get a prominent position early and ran a fine race to finish third.

Conduit was another with a double-figure draw to overcome, and he tended to race a shade keenly. He had

187

been beaten over five lengths by Sea The Stars in the Eclipse, but he's a proper 1m4f horse, at his best running on late from off a strong pace at this trip, so it was no surprise he got closer.

Dar Re Mi, moral winner of the Prix Vermeille on her previous start, confirmed her status as Europe's top middle-distance filly on her first outing against the colts, enjoying a dream run through the race and gaining revenge of sorts on Stacelita, who had been awarded the Vermeille in controversial circumstances.

Fame And Glory, beaten by Sea The Stars in the Derby and the Irish Champion, was back at his ideal trip, but the decision of the others to ignore the gallop set by his stable's two pacemakers compromised his chance. He was keen early and, in stark contrast to Sea The Stars, took a while to pick up in the straight

La Boum ran well for a 500-1 shot, but it is her relative proximity, and that of fellow outsiders Magadan and Tangaspeed, that inevitably limits the rating Sea The Stars was awarded here.

LONGCHAMP (R-H)
Sunday, October 4

OFFICIAL GOING: Good

6526a	QATAR PRIX DE L'ARC DE TRIOMPHE (GROUP 1) (C&F)	1m 4f

3:15 (3:17) 3-Y-O **£2,219,029** (£887,767; £443,883; £221,748; £111,068)

RPR

1		**Sea The Stars (IRE)**[29] 5688 3-8-11 .... MJKinane 6	132+

(John M Oxx, Ire) *lw: t.k.h: restrained after 1f and sn dropped to 9th: gd prog on inner 2f out: led just over 1f out and qcknd clr: impressive* **4/6**[1]

2	2	**Youmzain (IRE)**[28] 5707 6-9-5 ....(v) KFallon 1	125

(M R Channon) *broke wl: settled in mid-div: 11th st: clsng up fr over 2f out: qcknd through gap 1 1/2f out: drvn to take 2nd wl ins fnl f* **20/1**

3	hd	**Cavalryman**[21] 5930 3-8-11 .... LDettori 19	125

(A Fabre, France) *w'like: lw: sn prom: 5th st: drvn 2f out: 4th 1f out: 2nd 100yds out: kpt on steadily u.p* **12/1**

4	hd	**Conduit (IRE)**[71] 4298 4-9-5 .... RyanMoore 12	124

(Sir Michael Stoute) *mid-div: 10th st: stdy prog fnl 2f: tk 4th cl home* **8/1**[3]

5	1	**Dar Re Mi**[21] 5929 4-9-2 .... JimmyFortune 2	119

(J H M Gosden) *lw: first to show: racd in 4th to st: disp 2nd over 1f out: 2nd 150yds out: one pce* **25/1**

6	1	**Fame And Glory**[29] 5688 3-8-11 .... JMurtagh 10	121

(A P O'Brien, Ire) *plld early: 6th and racing keenly 1/2-way: 8th st: styd on one pce fnl 2f: nvr able to chal* **6/1**[2]

7	1/2	**La Boum (GER)**[42] 5300 6-9-2 .... TJarnet 8	117

(Robert Collet, France) *towards rr to st: swtchd outside 1 1/2f out: styd on: nvr a factor* **500/1**

7	dht	**Stacelita (FR)**[21] 5929 3-8-8 .... CSoumillon 16	117

(J-C Rouget, France) *leggy: racd in 3rd ldng main gp: 3rd st: led wl over 1f: hdd just over 1f out: one pce* **20/1**

9	3/4	**Magadan (IRE)**[98] 3443 4-9-5 .... ACrastus 17	119

(E Lellouche, France) *towards rr to st: sme prog on outside fnl 2f: nvr a factor* **150/1**

10	1/2	**Vision D'Etat (FR)**[21] 5931 4-9-5 .... OPeslier 9	118

(E Libaud, France) *a.p: 6th st: drvn over 1f out: one pce fnl f* **14/1**

11	3/4	**Tangaspeed (FR)**[21] 5929 4-9-2 .... IMendizabal 11	114

(R Laplanche, France) *last early: styd on u.str.p fnl 1 1/2f: nvr a factor* **500/1**

12	shd	**Beheshtam (FR)**[21] 5930 3-8-11 .... GMosse 15	117

(A De Royer-Dupre, France) *w'like: scope: lw: mid-div: 7th st: one pce fnl 2f* **16/1**

13	3	**Getaway (GER)**[28] 5707 6-9-5 .... SPasquier 3	112+

(J Hirschberger, Germany) *14th 1/2-way: tried to get through on ins of wnr over 2f out: drvn and hdwy over 1f out: nt clr run ins fnl f: eased* **33/1**

14	snk	**The Bogberry (USA)**[28] 5712 4-9-5 .... MKappushev 18	112

(A De Royer-Dupre, France) *a towards rr* **250/1**

15	8	**Hot Six (BRZ)**[63] 4-9-4 .... TJPereira 4	98

(G Duarte, Brazil) *bhd and rdn st: nvr a factor* **250/1**

16	2	**Tullamore (USA)**[63] 4-9-5 .... VJanacek 13	96

(Z Koplik, Czech Republic) *a bhd* **500/1**

17	4	**Grand Ducal (IRE)**[29] 5688 3-8-11 .... PJSmullen 5	89

(A P O'Brien, Ire) *sn led: hdd after 2f: 2nd st: wknd qckly wl over 1f out* **300/1**

18	2	**Set Sail (IRE)**[29] 5688 3-8-11 .... SMLevey 14	86

(A P O'Brien, Ire) *led after 2f to wl over 1f out: wknd qckly* **500/1**

19	15	**Steele Tango (USA)**[92] 3640 4-9-5 .... DarryllHolland 7	62

(R A Teal) *a bhd: last st: t.o* **500/1**

2m 26.3s (-4.10) **Going Correction** +0.15s/f (Good)
WFA 3 from 4yo+ 7lb   **19** Ran   SP% **124.7**
Speed ratings: 119,117,117,117,116 116,115,115,115,114 114,114,112,112,106
105,102,101,91
PARI-MUTUEL: WIN 1.80; PL 1.40, 3.30, 3.70; DF 14.30.
Owner Christopher Tsui **Bred** Sunderland Holdings **Trained** Currabeg, Co Kildare

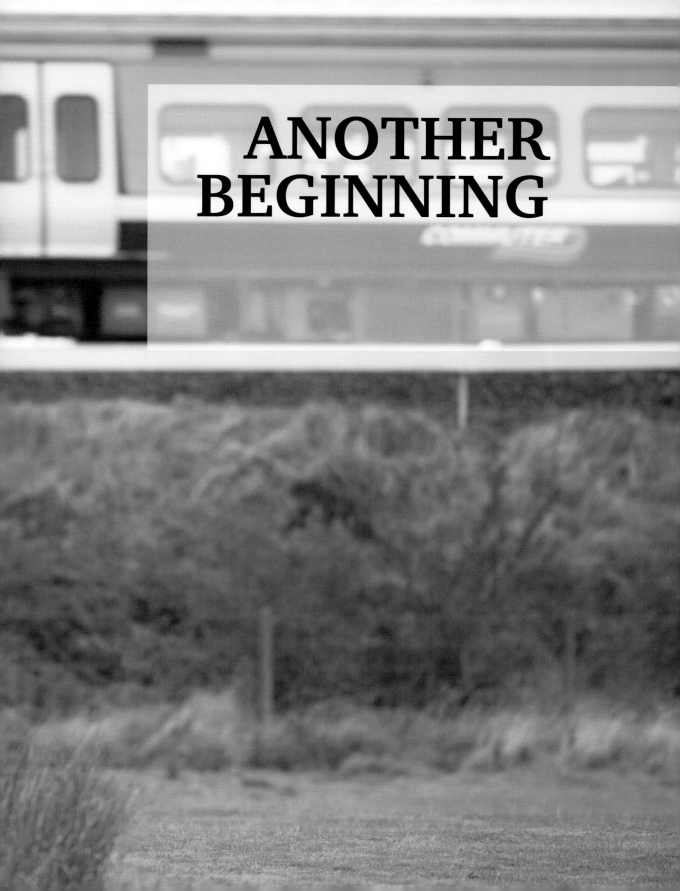

ANOTHER
BEGINNING

The day after the Arc, the headline in the Irish Times read: 'MOVE OVER ARKLE – THERE'S A NEW IRISH STAR ON THE HORIZON.' Racing correspondent Brian O'Connor's story began: 'Arkle has always been the most popular symbol of Irish racing excellence but the totemic steeplechaser now looks to have competition on his hands in the "legendary stakes" after Sea The Stars put the seal on a perfect season with victory in yesterday's Prix de l'Arc de Triomphe in Paris.'

Invoking the spirit of Arkle was appropriate, for scarcely had Sea The Stars pulled up at Longchamp than the slide rules had been produced and experts were forming into gaggles to try and measure exactly where to position Sea The Stars in the rankings of the all-time great racehorses – whereas, as with Arkle, the true measure of his greatness was the effect which the horse had on people.

Throughout this book there has been evidence of how Sea The Stars touched the lives both of those close to him and those who turned up at the racecourse or watched on television to marvel at him. And as with so many other aspects of the Sea The Stars story, the wisest and most telling words come from his trainer John Oxx:

'I couldn't have imagined I'd have a horse like this: nobody has the right to think they could have a horse like this. My father was a great reader, a great student. He bought every horse book, and he used to sit me down when I was a kid and read about the greatest horses of thoroughbred history, and he was always telling me about the great horses like Arkle and all those horses before I was born. When you're a kid, life is so simple, and I'd be thinking, "Ah, some day I'll train one of those." And then you start training, and ten years down the line you think, "This isn't so easy", and then maybe you get a very good horse, and you think he's great but he really isn't, and you start to realise that you'll never get one of the true greats.

Previous spread: *Winding down after the Arc, Sea The Stars takes his morning stroll with Alex da Silva.*

So to have a horse like this, one of the undisputed greats, is just
unbelievable – a miracle.

'It's marvellous to think that we've had him here and we've
managed to succeed with him. But those great horses make it
easy: they're great and that's it. You know that if you don't make
a mess of it, they'll come through.

'Nobody can know who the greatest horse is, but certainly
this fellow is the most complete horse that could be bred at the
moment. If you resurrected all the great horses from the past
and put them standing up there in front of you and walked
them up and down and looked at them, and at their pedigrees,
their performance, their race record, their temperament, their
conformation and everything, you'd pick some holes in every
horse. But you'd have a difficulty picking a hole with this fellow.
He's got the pedigree, the looks, that tremendous athletic frame,
the temperament and then the record. When you put it all
together, no breeder could hope to breed a better horse 300 years
down the line from the development of the thoroughbred, and
that's what he represents to me: the ultimate development of the
thoroughbred species now, in 2009. Would Sea-Bird would have
beaten him in an Arc? We don't know; nobody knows. But as a
whole package Sea The Stars is just the ultimate.'

In the days following the Arc, Racing Post *writers offered*
their own opinions of how Sea The Stars should be ranked …

A horse who is always better than the bare result

JAMES WILLOUGHBY
5 October 2005

SEA THE STARS' victory at Longchamp told us little more than we already knew about his merit. This is a horse who is always better than the bare result – full stop.

Whatever figure handicappers put on him cannot do him justice. He defies accurate assessment because he has proved so much better than any other horse who has challenged him.

From a technical standpoint, yesterday's race was thoroughly unsatisfactory. The field ignored the two Aidan O'Brien pacemakers – who did little more than provide a bizarre sideshow – and there was a lot of bunching in the pack as a result.

The main race behind the pacemakers followed a slow-fast-slow pattern, with the final 400m of 23.8sec slower than in the four Group 1s which came before it. The sectionals here are for the leader at each point of the race and disguise the effort made by the pack running into the straight, which took its toll in the end.

Had Sea The Stars not idled, he might have completed the final 200m faster than 11.9sec, but it still would not have been anything like the same split registered by the other great horses on their best days. That was just the run of the race and takes nothing away from Sea The Stars.

Sea The Stars has already achieved some remarkable feats against the clock, of course, and it is his ability to sustain a sequence of these efforts which defines him – far more than any single performance.

PRIX DE L'ARC DE TRIOMPHE SECTIONAL TIMES:

TIME: 2min 26.3sec
SECTIONS:
2,400-1,000m: 85.6
1,000-600m: 24.0
600-400m: 12.9
400-200m: 11.9
200m-finish: 11.9

Fears that he might suffer trouble in the big field or might be caught out by the effects of a long campaign looked valid at one point, for Sea The Stars pulled hard even for him and also was momentarily in a position from which he might not have recovered if a horse had unexpectedly come back on top of him.

But further inspection of the iso-camera film revealed those fears were largely the product of anxiety on the watcher's part. But for having to shut out Getaway's ambitious attempt to squeeze up his inner early in the straight, then needing a seam to open soon after, Sea The Stars was probably in more control than his observers.

In truth, there wasn't a horse in the field with the push-button acceleration to trouble him. Though six Group 1 winners followed him home, the frame was filled by Youmzain, Cavalryman and Conduit, who are not horses with top-notch stalk-and-pounce ability.

It is nice to think that Sea The Stars is the best horse ever, but the nature of racing doesn't allow those comparisons to have real credibility. All that can be said is that he has earned a place among the greats; but let's be honest, he did not have Sea-Bird or Dancing Brave coming at him, nor did he have the chance to run a time to rival Peintre Celebre.

But Sea The Stars appeals to people on an emotional level, not because of the horses he has beaten or the acceleration he has shown, but because he is so complete. He is seemingly unconquerable and indefatigable, imperious and unflappable; he just cannot be shaken by rival or by circumstance.

And that is the trigger for awe. We see so many thousands of horses every year, even good ones, who can't shake off bad luck or are humbled by the run of the race; they might be unable to keep up the gallop or be caught short of a turn of foot.

But nothing bothers this horse, or at least it hasn't yet. There is only one rival who has the raw ability to run with him, but he, Rip Van Winkle, is compromised by infirmity.

The possible rematch between the two in the Breeders' Cup Classic may not have the purity it should because of the unfamiliar surface, but there is a good chance that it may even exceed yesterday's race because Rip Van Winkle is now in better shape than when Sea The Stars last beat him – and is a better horse than the vanquished at Longchamp.

Out on the Curragh.

I, for one, hope we have seen the last of this amazing horse

ALASTAIR DOWN

6 October 2009

PARIS on the Monday morning after the Arc and with beneficent timing the rains have come – after Sea The Stars has safely done his stuff on ground infinitely better than is the norm at Longchamp in October.

Never before in the anxious hours before a major race have I been so struck by a crowd's single and united desire, almost a longing, that nothing would go wrong and that the favourite would win. The power of reason and the evidence of form books have a curious way of weakening at the end of a long season and many a great has come to the Arc only to find it like the bridge at Arnhem – a race too far.

And though this physical one-off has continued to astonish with his wellbeing, weight and strength, John Oxx's every antenna will have been quivering daily for the first, slightest inkling that enough was enough.

I, for one, hope we have seen the last of this remarkable horse. Those who wish to see him in the Breeders' Cup at Santa Anita doubtless mean well (or have already booked) but on 7 November ,Sea The Stars should be pottering about the edge of the Curragh communing with a passing sheep and being brought steadily off the mental and physical treadmill on which he has been since the beginning of the year.

Of course a Breeders' Cup triumph would be memorable,

FRANKIE DETTORI

'He's a great horse, he's beaten everything put in front of him, has been a privilege to race against and is one of the greats.'

but it would be Group 1 month seven, he would be travelling for the first time to another time zone, a different climate and it would surely be the first unreasonable question asked of him.

One wonders what it must have been like for everyone at Oxx's yard to have this phenomenon living and breathing among them? How many times must Oxx have paraphrased Humphrey Bogart in Casablanca and asked: 'Of all the gin joints in all the world and he walks into mine.' And while in Casablanca mode I might add, thank God, that 'We'll always have Paris.'

It is not just Oxx who has enjoyed this season of magic but every lad and lass in the place. They will all have fussed over him, touched greatness and been touched by it in turn.

In their old age they will have the summer of '09 about which to reminisce.

Make no mistake, the benchmark for the 21st-century racehorse has been set here, even though we are just nine years into the hundred.

Every yard gets a buzz from a good horse, but Sea The Stars is now in the ring fighting for the title of the greatest ever. Personally I am always a little uncomfortable with the apparent need to establish a definitive pecking order; it always strikes me as a bit like comparing your children with each other.

All I can say is that in my lifetime only Sea-Bird and Brigadier Gerard have any claims to be superior and in the Brigadier's case he would have been all at sea against this star over a mile and a half.

With speculation rife as to where Sea The Stars will stand at stud it is worth noting that Sea-Bird can charitably be described as a disappointment at stud while the Brigadier, God bless him, was an absolute shocker as a stallion and his descendants had to be crossed with the drays from Whitbreads to inject some speed into them.

What is fascinating about Sea The Stars is how nobody has yet come up with a major flaw or failing about him. Most horses have quirks: the great St Simon hated cats and would kill any that came within reach, while Montjeu, for all his physical talents, was clearly a splendid assortment of psychological complaints as well.

In addition to his magnificence as a physical specimen, Sea The Stars is that rare horse whose temperament has made a deep impression for all the right reasons. He is dependable not deranged, benevolent not bonkers, ever calm and never crazy.

It will be fascinating to see where he stands and who emerges as the owners of the lion's shares. Relations between Coolmore and the Tsui family have not been without their fluctuations and it is certain that Sheikh Mohammed will be mad keen to have a major say in Sea The Stars as a stallion.

Perhaps the Tsui family will try to paddle their own canoe but one thing is certain, no horse in my lifetime will have gone to stud with so many perfect tens from the judges of conformation, form book and temperament.

As for the racecourse, it is time to bring the curtain down. At last I fully understand the words of *Cwm Rhondda*, greatest of hymns, the mighty lines of which run: Bread of Heaven, Bread of Heaven, Feed me till I want no more …

The feast of Sea The Stars has been enough for any and every man. Now he can pass unsullied into legend and *Cwm Rhondda* says it all once more: Songs of Praises, Songs of Praises, I will ever give to thee, I will ever give to thee …

ALAIN DE ROYER-DUPRE

'He is among those exceptional horses who make their mark at the highest level of competition. At Longchamp, he impressed me with his physical appearance. He was magnificent.'

199

The Raceform view

GRAHAM DENCH

SO where does Sea The Stars stand among the all-time greats? Judged by conventional handicapping methods, it would be hard to rate him as highly as the legendary Sea-Bird, or for that matter those giants of the 1970s, Nijinsky, Brigadier Gerard and Mill Reef, for his style of racing and his tendency to idle in front meant that he did not win by extravagant margins; indeed he never won by further than two and a half lengths.

It's not hard to envisage either Nijinsky or Brigadier Gerard beating Delegator every bit as easily in the Guineas, while Sea-Bird, Nijinsky or Mill Reef would surely have overcome the Ballydoyle horses as effectively as Sea The Stars did in the Derby. Similarly one would imagine Sea Bird or Mill Reef would have beaten Youmzain and company in the Arc, even if they had faced the obstacles Sea The Stars had to overcome.

However, the figures suggest Sea The Stars would have been more than a match for just about any horse since then, quite possibly even Dancing Brave, and his Leopardstown mark of 138 places him joint top turf performer with Daylami since the Racing Post Ratings service began in 1988, and just ahead of Generous, Peintre Celebre and Zilzal. What's more, he was head and shoulders above his contemporaries in what was widely recognised to be a particularly good year, one with real strength in depth.

Perhaps that's not the point though. Would Sea-Bird, Nijinsky, Brigadier Gerard, Mill Reef or any of the other outstanding thoroughbreds that have graced the turf have been capable of attaining such a high standard again and again throughout such a demanding campaign, one in which there was never the opportunity to enjoy one of the soft options that were relatively commonplace 30 or 40 years ago?

And has there been a more perfect example of the modern thoroughbred? Sea The Stars had it all. The foundations of his excellence were his beautiful breeding, faultless conformation, solid constitution and superb temperament. Nurtured with consummate skill by John Oxx, campaigned boldly by Christopher Tsui, and ridden exquisitely by Mick Kinane, he went on to display all the attributes we most desire in a racehorse, showing an unsurpassed blend of speed, stamina, courage, athleticism and versatility as he strode unbeaten through six successive Group 1 wins.

It is debatable if we have ever seen his like before. It is doubtful if we will ever see his like again.

* * *

Sea The Stars had finished racing in Europe, but there were still two major loose ends to tie up: would he go to Santa Anita for the Breeders' Cup Classic in early November, and where would he stand at stud?

The answer to the first appeared in the Racing Post *on Wednesday 14 October, ten days after the Arc, under the front-page headline, 'FAREWELL TO A LEGEND'. To nobody's great surprise, Sea The Stars would not be making the trip to California. John Oxx admitted that the massive prize money for the Classic had been a consideration, but not one strong enough to lure the Tsuis: 'It was a temptation with all that prize money and such an important race meeting and important race, and also the fact that the horse was so well after the Arc. But at the same time, I thought it was a step too far. Originally we were more inclined to think of the Breeders' Cup as his final race if he had missed the Arc had the ground been unsuitable in France, as then we could have eased him up a bit in his work.*

'It was more of an alternative to the Arc rather than seriously thinking of going for both of them, so it wasn't really a tough decision.'

And the resolution of the second major loose end was announced in the Racing Post *before the end of October:*

Stars will stand at Aga's Irish stud and cover Zarkava

NANCY SEXTON

28 October 2009

SEA THE STARS will begin his stallion career next year at the Aga Khan's Gilltown Stud in County Kildare, where one of his first mates will be last season's Arc heroine Zarkava.

Since the colt's retirement was announced two weeks ago, speculation as to where the multiple Group 1-winning son of Cape Cross will stand has been rife, with the Irish National Stud, Kildangan Stud and Plantation Stud in Newmarket mooted as possibilities alongside Gilltown.

After the Arc: Mick Kinane still in the media spotlight.

Sea The Stars will stand his first season alongside Dalakhani and Azamour at a fee of €85,000 and is likely to arrive at Gilltown from John Oxx's Currabeg yard 'sooner rather than later', according to stud manager Pat Downes.

Ling Tsui, mother of the colt's owner Christopher Tsui, said in a statement: 'His Highness was kind enough to let us stand Sea The Stars at Gilltown while keeping ownership of him, and we are most grateful. The staff and facilities at Gilltown are top class and Sea The Stars will enjoy his stay there.'

Although Sea The Stars' departure from Currabeg marks the end of an era for Oxx, the trainer expressed his relief at the development, saying: 'It's nice that a home has been found for him, and the sooner he's out in the paddocks the better, because you get a bit nervous when they're about to go.

'The Aga Khan was over to see something with us in the late summer and he saw Sea The Stars then, as everybody would want to do. They [the Tsuis] were always going to stand him in Ireland. They never had any intention to sell, and narrowed down the list. I wasn't involved in the discussions. My job was to train him, and his owners were well capable of negotiating on this, so I left it to them.'

The Aga Khan has already enjoyed success with several homebreds by Sea The Stars' half brother Galileo, including recent Prix du Cadran winner Alandi, and is understandably delighted with the addition to his roster.

He said: 'Mrs Tsui and Christopher's decision to entrust the future career at stud of Sea The Stars to Gilltown Stud farm brings to everyone at the Aga Khan Studs, as well as to me personally, the greatest happiness.

'Mrs Tsui and Christopher's decision is certainly one of the most important developments for my operation since I inherited it in 1960.

'This horse could also help develop relations to bring Chinese investment into the European bloodstock market.'

CHRISTOPHE LEMAIRE

'I think Sea The Stars almost represents perfection. He is what all breeders are looking to produce. The colt has the perfect physique, temperament, action and quality. In fact, he appears to have no faults.'

CLARE BALDING

'He is certainly the greatest horse I have seen, given that I was born the year Mill Reef started doing his stuff. I realise that those who have been around longer will make arguments for other horses. I think he had a wonderful combination of talent, acceleration, soundness and unbelievable temperament, and also that movie-star quality – he knew he was special.'

The Aga's views were echoed by Downes, who said: 'It's great for the Irish breeding industry that he's standing in Ireland. It's hard to find any weakness in him. I saw him train on the Curragh many times, so I'm very familiar with him.'

The details of Sea The Stars' first book of mares will be finalised at a later date, but an early selection is the Aga Khan's own unbeaten champion Zarkava, who signed off her seven-race career with a victory in last year's Arc. The daughter of Zamindar is in foal to fellow Arc winner Dalakhani.

'In keeping with the motto of the Aga Khan Studs "Success breeds success", I look forward to the earliest opportunity to send my unbeaten champion Zarkava to Sea The Stars,' said the Aga Khan.

'I believe the last two Arc winners were made for each other in terms of ability, temperament and conformation. The best needs to be bred to the best.'

The exact size of Sea The Stars' first book has also yet to be finalised, but Dalakhani covered 120 mares last spring and it is more than likely Sea The Stars will follow suit.

'Our stallions don't cover very big books,' said Downes. 'Dalakhani covered 120 mares this year and we would be inclined to follow the same pattern with Sea The Stars.

'It's wonderful that all breeders can access him. He will fit most mares, although it's too early to say exactly how many of the Aga Khan's he will cover.'

Opposite: *On 29 October 2009, John Lynes delivers Sea The Stars to his new home at Gilltown Stud.*

One enterprising bookmaker immediately offered odds of 50-1 that the first offspring of Sea The Stars and Zarkava would win the Triumph Hurdle at Cheltenham.

His is a memory we too are proud to cheer

BROUGH SCOTT

THE journey Sea The Stars had to make on Thursday 29 October was not a long one. The trip east across the Curragh plain from John Oxx's stables to the Aga Khan's Gilltown Stud near Kilcullen would take less than half an hour and end him within 10 miles of his birthplace. But the voyage he now embarks on as a stallion is endless. If he is successful he can be a fountainhead down the ages.

In that lies both the fault and the fascination in top-class Flat racing. For the sports fan, the new champion has streaked through the classic season like some blazing comet which has passed before the world has fully realised that it was there at all. For the purist, the endless debate as to exactly where he fits in the pantheon continues on down the generations, and within just three years we start to see his progeny on the track.

For the fascination to hold we must garner the memories. At *Racing Post* we have a team uniquely equipped to do just that. It has been my special pleasure that after a life which has witnessed Ribot, Sea Bird, Nijinsky, Mill Reef and Dancing Brave, I have now got close to a horse who achieved something beyond even those heroes of yesteryear. His is a memory we too are proud to cheer.

SEA THE STARS' CAREER IN SUMMARY

LEFT TO RIGHT: date; course; going; race name (with Pattern status in parentheses); distance in furlongs; jockey; starting price (UK industry price in the case of the Qatar Prix de l'Arc de Triomphe); finishing position; prize money in £ sterling or at the prevailing exchange rate.

2008

Date	Course	Going	Race	Dist	Jockey	SP	Pos	Prize
13 July	Curragh	good	Jebel Ali Stables & Racecourse EBF Maiden	7	MJ Kinane	6-1	4th	£455.88
17 Aug	Leopardstown	soft/heavy	Korean Racing Authority EBF Maiden	7	MJ Kinane	2-1F	WON	£9,573.53
28 Sept	Curragh	yielding	Juddmonte Beresford Stakes (Gp2)	8	MJKinane	7-4	WON	£59,742.65

2009

Date	Course	Going	Race	Dist	Jockey	SP	Pos	Prize
2 May	Newmarket	good/firm	Stanjames.co, 2,000 Guineas (Gp1)	8	MJ Kinane	8-1	WON	£241,840.20
6 June	Epsom Downs	good	Investec Derby (Gp1)	12	MJ Kinane	11-4	WON	£709,625.00
4 July	Sandown Park	good	Coral-Eclipse Stakes (Gp1)	10	MJ Kinane	4-7F	WON	£283,850.00
18 Aug	York	good/firm	Juddmonte International Stakes (Gp1)	10.5	MJ Kinane	1-4F	WON	£340,620.00
5 Sept	Leopardstown	good/yielding	Tattersalls Millions Irish Champion Stakes (Gp1)	10	MJ Kinane	4-6F	WON	£552,427.18
4 Oct	Longchamp	good	Qatar Prix de l'Arc de Triomphe (Gp1)	12	MJ Kinane	4-6F	WON	£2,219,029.00

SEA THE STARS

- raced nine times, winning eight
- was ridden in all his races by Mick Kinane
- ran four races in England, four races in Ireland, and one in France
- earned £4,417,163 in prize money
- covered 10.5 miles in his nine races
- raced for 17mins 36.2sec
- longest price: 8-1 in 2009 StanJames.com 2,000 Guineas
- shortest price: 1-4 in 2009 Juddmonte International Stakes
- longest winning distance: 2½ lengths in 2008 Korean Racing Authority EBF Maiden and 2009 Tattersalls Millions Irish Champion Stakes
- shortest winning distance: ½ length in 2008 Juddmonte Beresford Stakes
- in six races in 2009, Aidan O'Brien fielded 12 different horses, a total of 19 runners, in an unavailing attempt to lower the Sea The Stars colours